SERIOUS DREAMS

DREAMS

BOLD IDEAS FOR THE
REST OF YOUR LIFE

EDITED BY **BYRON BORGER**

In Christian art, the square halo identified a living person presumed to be a saint. Square Halo Books is devoted to publishing works that present contextually sensitive biblical studies and practical instruction consistent with the Doctrines of the Reformation. The goal of Square Halo Books is to provide materials useful for encouraging and equipping the saints.

First Edition 2015

Copyright ©2015 Square Halo Books
P.O. Box 18954, Baltimore, MD 21206
ISBN 978-1-941106-01-3
Oak forest cover photo credit: bernjuer / photocase.com

CONTENTS

LIVE WELL
DO GOOD
BE TRUE

Dedicated to my colleagues, past
and present, of the CCO. They pour themselves
out for college students, inviting them to
visions of the Jubilee—the very shalom of God—
and into visions of vocation, year after year.
And to those who musician Matt Kearney calls the
"heartbreak dreamers." It's gonna be all right.

BYRON BORGER

It's funny how, when somebody seems destined for great things in our culture, we say, "She is really going to go far," as if there is great virtue in leaving home, moving away, heading out to, well, anywhere but here. It is almost a cliché that young adults who move back to their old hometowns (let alone to their childhood houses) are losers. After all, who doesn't want to "go far?"

Yet there is also another set of voices these days calling us to stay put, live locally, celebrate the small and mundane, form communities, and discover vibrant ways of finding home in a culture of displacement.

Graduation speeches—and, at first glance, maybe even

the speeches in this little volume—tend towards the first view. "Oh, the places you'll go," the great Dr. Seuss predicted. Who isn't inspired by the encouraging word to really "make something of yourself?" In some Christian circles, much is made about God's call to change the world and our mandate to transform the culture. I like that breathy, exciting rhetoric—you'll see it in my own speech, I hope. But such an attitude can be damaging. So allow me to say here at the outset that there is nothing wrong with staying put. We don't have to go far; we don't really have to go anywhere new or different or big. In fact, many of our wisest writers here in the hot-wired, fast-paced, twenty-first century do not invite us to the highest paying jobs, to the glitz of the big city, or to halls of power and prestige. Rather, they invite us to quiet, ordinary lives in small towns, caring for extended family and friends—not "going far," but staying home.

From the esteemed Kentucky farmer, novelist, poet, and essayist, Wendell Berry, we are inspired to develop a sense of place, caring about local regions, watersheds, rural places. From Presbyterian pastor and writer Eugene Peterson, we hear the themes of paying attention to local details, practicing the presence of God in the ordinary and the mundane. Books like the one by Jonathan Wilson-Hartgrove drawing on old monastic wisdom called *The Wisdom of Stability: Rooting Faith in a Mobile Culture* praise the value of steadiness. Stability may not sound that enticing to a fresh-out-of-college young adult like you, but for those who are serious about living into the contours of a meaningful, good life after college, stability is important to consider alongside the louder calls to "go big or go home." Maybe part of what it may mean for you to live well and do good is to be true to your own hometown.

Maybe you will be inspired by these energetic speeches to head out into the world and be used by God for Christ's Kingdom's sake, and that might take you to faraway cities and exciting, innovative jobs. But I hope you will also consider what Steve Garber calls "common grace for the common good"—which is a pretty big idea—that God cares about common graces built into creation such as good friends, healthy food, imaginative art, sustainable neighborhoods, helpful stores, nourishing families, trusted spouses. God is at work in many small, ordinary, human things such as work and play and art and citizenship, and we are invited by God to cultivate these common gifts, for the good of all. Our salvation in Christ is for this very purpose: to live humanly in the world that God loves, so that we, our neighbors, and our neighborhoods may flourish. Few people say this better than Amy Sherman, whose inspiring chapter reminds us that our success is for the sake of the broader community.

This big vision of the common good is often lived out in small ways. But these exciting talks delivered with great passion on days given to celebrate commencements could be misunderstood as a call only to go big, to go far. They should not be misunderstood, as if we are calling you only to extraordinarily great things.

Don't feel bad for getting an ordinary job with a plain-sounding title and an unremarkable salary in your major which, maybe for you, was a mixed-bag, anyway. You don't even have to feel bad for getting an ordinary job that is not in your major! That's just the way it works sometimes.

Yes, most of us long to see the world healed and made a bit more whole. We want our own professions and workplaces to be transformed so they are better, healthier, serving the world in the way they should. Many of us long to play a part in the redemptive story of God. There is nothing good about living a boring life—what Thoreau called "quiet desperation." But this call to find a life of purpose and joy by taking up our vocations in the world doesn't necessarily mean doing big, crazy things. We don't have to be extraordinary. We can, as the Bible sometimes says, live quiet and peaceful lives, blooming gracefully where we are planted, learning to care and mature in ordinary discipleship.

As elder social justice activist and leader in the cause of racial reconciliation, Dr. John Perkins, reminds us in his challenging graduation speech offered at Seattle Pacific University, "you have enough to learn more." I think he meant that, as college graduates, you have learned how to learn, to think well, to study, to develop your own personal library, to figure stuff out. You have the skills and self-discipline and habits of heart that will allow you to continue being life-long learners. You will continue to grow and thrive. You will need to because this "making a difference" stuff, whether in a posh office at a Fortune 500 company or in returning to a familiar summer job for a season or two, takes time.

Graduation speeches are naturally designed to be inspiring, motivational, upbeat. We really can be salt and light and leaven; we can be in the world and not of it; we can make a difference. In the power of the Holy Spirit, we really can be transformed into agents of God's coming Kingdom. But it may or may not entail big time passion, and super-radical lifestyles. More likely, you'll just put one foot ahead of the other, day by day by day, *soli deo gloria.*

It takes time to get your bearings, to find your sweet spot. And that is my point in these introductory remarks. We hope these talks encourage you, inspire you, remind you of some key themes you most likely have heard over the years of your college career. This *is* an exciting time in your life, even if bittersweet. But don't feel badly if you don't see yourself as a "change agent" and "radical Christian" who "makes a difference" right away. We all have to lean into these things, be patient with ourselves, and learn more about the spiritual practices that will sustain us over the long haul. You've gotten through college. The silly little slogan on plaques and posters and cards really is true—today actually is the first day of the rest of your life. I think these meditations and reflections will keep you moving forward. Live well, do good, be true.

So, I've danced around two themes that might help frame or inform your reading of these graduation messages. Let me be clear: first, you don't have to "go far" or really "make something of yourself." You may be called to less dramatic, more mundane faithfulness, serving God and nurturing your faith in pedestrian ways in places that don't look like a TV show. Not all of us can be social entrepreneurs who start new charities or websites or programs or protests. Starting up a start-up isn't for everyone. Changing the world may even be, as Eugene Cho put it in a book by this title, overrated. It's okay to be ordinary.

Secondly, we have to be patient as we step into our lives' vocations. We may know we are called to be part of God's redemptive mission and that that is the story that shapes our lives. But, like everyone else, we have to learn the skills and craft and practices of our professions. We have to, as the saying goes, earn the right to be heard. We have to be life-long learners, deepening our insight and fidelity to our call-ings, our jobs, our places and relationships. Whether we are called to the high-power corporate world in a cool urbane setting or a less prestigious job in a small town, we have to do the work, learning day by day. These speeches will be good reminders of the bigger picture, even serving as provocative commissionings to see your life as part of the Biblical story of the all-of-life-redeemed Kingdom coming. All of these speeches invite you to fresh thinking and renewed commit-ments to joining God in your careers and callings. You've got a lot of baby steps to take in this season of your life, and that's okay. God is gracious, and you can take your time.

Another important theme that is hinted at in several of these reflections needs to be named here, too. Nicholas Wolterstorff talks movingly about having eyes that shed tears, and reminds us of the Bible's invitation to "weep with those who weep." John Perkins teaches from the Good Samaritan story about the Jericho Road where an unnamed person had empathy, the first attribute of a life of com-passion. Claudia Beversluis reminds you that "when your gut aches and your heart breaks" you should "find a place to share the pain." I think that anyone who is going to maintain visions of vocation and be faithful in small things for God's glory will have to become a person who is not afraid of shedding tears. As the late and still beloved contemplative writer Henri Nouwen put it, we must become "wounded healers." The Bible is full of those who experienced hardships, mystery, confusion, hurt, tears, rage, and lament. To not name our fears and doubts is denial. We who want to develop a Christian worldview and care about the things God cares about in the very way God cares about them, simply must be prepared to host our hurt. We must honestly attend to the great anxieties we have about our own lives and about the state of the world. Don't let anyone or anything (let alone these happy speeches inviting you to serve God in the years ahead) suggest that you can't be honest about your own heart.

It isn't the main theme of this collection, but it bears saying: if we try to struggle against the idols and dysfunctions and crude values of our culture, perhaps of our workplaces, maybe even of our own broken families, we will seem a bit counter-cultural. We may feel like weirdos because we care so deeply and are in touch with the brokenness of this fallen world. Art historian and Christian philosopher Calvin Seerveld, in a collection called *Biblical Studies & Wisdom for Living,* writes to some graduating seniors and reminds them that Jesus said His yoke would be light. "It fits well over your graduating shoulders," Seerveld, said, "even if it makes you feel maladjusted in our Darwinian survival-of-the-fittest society." It is okay to feel maladjusted.

This idea about being prepared for hard times is the climax of my own talk given to graduate students at Geneva College, and I hope you take it to heart. The black gospel tradition that inspired the civil rights movement can instruct us all in this matter. I mention Mahalia Jackson singing to Martin Luther King, Jr. over the phone in the middle of the night, "Precious Lord, take my hand."

If you are battered and bruised from trying to make a difference in the world, if you are sad and discouraged because you haven't found your niche or your calling, if you are full of frustration and doubt and anxiety, or if you've faced disheartening resistance to your fresh ideas for healthy reformation in your church or workplace, you can sing the many laments from the Bible with integrity. You can cry out to God through your tears and fears.

Our glad and hopeful speeches collected here offer congratulations and inspiration and emphasize God's desire for graduating seniors to take up their careers and vocations as holy callings. Each one of us deeply realizes that making the transition between Sunday and Monday, carrying faith into the work-world, market-place, and contemporary culture, is harder than it sounds. We know that we all have to cope with setbacks and anguish. We know from the Bible and the best thinking of Christian leaders throughout history, that this is normal; tears are nothing to be ashamed of.

A very creative writer who has experienced more than her share of anguish and who continues to give her life to others is Anne Lamott. In her lovely book *Stitches:*

A Handbook on Meaning, Hope and Repair, she writes,

> We connect with God in our humanity. A great truth, attributed to Emily Dickinson, is that "hope inspires the good to reveal itself." This is almost all I ever need to remember. Gravity and sadness yank us down, and hope gives us a nudge to help one another get back up or to sit with the fallen on the ground, in the abyss, in solidarity.

Most commencement speeches don't say this, but you shouldn't be surprised when "gravity and sadness" yank you down. Be prepared to lament, to be with others in your times of need, and to sit with others in their own abysses. A high priority for you in this post-college time is figuring out how to find and form supportive community, to maintain your best friendships, and to find a local church body whose members can walk with you in life's ups and downs.

Added to this collection of speeches is an epilogue by Erica Young Reitz who has served college students for many years. She has a book coming out, tentatively called *Life After College*, that will be about this time of young adult transitions. Erica's book will be both visionary and practical, aware of both the fresh opportunities and looming pitfalls of young adult faith development and post-college discipleship. Her brief remarks here are themselves an integral part of this book, and the stories she tells are going to be helpful for you. They will assist you in moving from the profound and glorious rhetoric of these messages to the daily steps you need to take in order to live into this stuff.

I know I speak for all the contributors who allowed us to use their commencement addresses when I say that we truly hope that the next season of your life will be very meaningful, and that, though tears may be shed at times, you come to know deep, deep joy. God cares about you, about all areas of your life, and there are very significant ways God invites you to think faithfully and serve well wherever you find yourself. Together with your friends and church, you will have to figure out what that looks like.

These chapters deserve repeated readings and can be good companions along the way as you, in the great line from the chapter by Claudia Beversluis, "make God and God's good news believable to others, not just through your words, but through the daily ways you live."

You really can live well, friends. You will surely do good. And please, be true, be faithful. Know, above all, that the God who loves you, who calls you, who has sustained you thus far, is true. God will be faithful—whether you go far or stay put.

A WORD
ABOUT
SPEECHES

These speeches were each given at real graduation ceremonies. Most were delivered at undergraduate commencements at Christian liberal arts colleges, one was delivered to graduate students, and another was offered to the graduating class of a seminary. Regardless of the sort of institution from which you graduated—or even if you didn't graduate, for that matter—these inspiring talks can help you on your way.

We edited out a few of the congratulatory comments at the start of each. The speakers, of course, named the college Presidents, thanked everybody on the dais, made nice with the Trustees. They are all earnestly polite and we wouldn't want you to think otherwise.

We did leave a number of the particularities of each speech intact, not to bore you with details of those specific places, with their own heroes and lingo and traditions, but because they were germane to the actual speech, and to illustrate that these were real talks, messages crafted for a certain group of people, in a particular place. That's how it often works: we lean in and listen to others, even if their locations and situations are a bit dissimilar to our own. Their storied specificity actually keeps us from being too abstract and lofty. Christian faith is always embodied, down to earth, real. We think these are good examples of that.

Of course these were originally spoken and heard, live. They were each delivered at real places and have that story-telling energy and sermonic style, but we think they are universal enough to be of great benefit, here in print, in mostly unedited form. We think that the largest story of which they speak—the gospel of Christ's Kingdom—comes through the details of these various places. We're sure you're smart enough to notice the instances where the unique setting shines through, and appreciate that for what it is: authenticity.

We give special thanks to these commencement speakers who allowed their words to be used in this volume. We are grateful for their generosity and their belief in this project. They all care deeply about the vocations of young adults and it was a delight to get to bring their good lines and significant insight to a broader audience.

WHAT
IT'S ALL
ABOUT

RICHARD J. MOUW

DELIVERED AT
MESSIAH COLLEGE
GRANTHAM, PENNSYLVANIA

Members of this new graduating class, congratulations to you for having arrived at this point in your journeys. It's a great honor for me to have this opportunity to express a few thoughts to you on this important occasion. But first, I want to make an announcement on behalf of the faculty and administration of the College:

> It has been Messiah's pleasure to serve you thus far. The school appreciates your business. The folks here at Messiah know you have a choice of colleges, and they thank you for choosing Messiah College. If your future plans should call for more

Christian higher education, we hope that you will think of Messiah College. And one more thing—be sure to be careful when opening the overhead compartments, because the contents may have shifted during your journey here.

This spoof of what you often hear on airplane trips these days is a way of making a serious point. I do hope the contents of your minds have shifted a bit because of what you have learned here. You have been exposed to some great ideas. You have read many assigned texts, written many papers and tests, studied film and other artistic expressions, learned about various patterns of professional service, done some experiments and field projects. And all of that was designed by this world-class faculty to rearrange the contents of your minds—even adding some things to those contents.

If all of that has worked in you in the way it was intended, then you have gained the capacity for significant critical reflection on important matters. And that is a good thing. I hope you will continue to cultivate a robust intellectual life.

DuringtheyearswhenIwasteachinginanundergraduate philosophy department, one of my senior departmental colleagues was a great storyteller. One of his delightful tales—he insisted that this really happened—was about a conversation that he claimed to have overheard between two women students who were talking in the hallway outside his office. His door was slightly ajar, so he could hear what they were saying—especially since the conversation was quite impassioned. The boyfriend of one of the young women had just broken up with her, and she was very distraught, sobbing loudly. Her friend was attempting to comfort her, but none of her therapeutic strategies seemed to be working. Finally, the would-be counselor made a bold pastoral move. "Look," she said to her grieving friend, "you've just got to be *philosophical* about this!"

"What do you mean?" the distraught young woman asked through her tears.

Her friend replied, "Just don't *think* about it!"

Needless to say, that is not the way we faculty types see our task. We try to get students to think carefully about important questions. So, on behalf of your teachers, I have to encourage you to continue to think about significant things—the kinds of significant things that have been very much on the academic agenda during your time here.

But I also hope that you will be always clear about what this is really all about: that this thinking, as well as the other kinds of sensitivities and concerns that have come into your lives during these courses of study, will always be directed toward the most important goal for any Christian—that is the goal of bringing glory to God by promoting the cause of Christ's Kingdom.

Men and women of this new graduating class, the world desperately needs people who are gifted with the ability to think carefully about the basic issues of life. And for all of the complex thinking to which we are called as people who have been privileged to participate in this great project of Christian liberal arts education, it really comes down to some rather simple things in the end. But the simplicity must be, for the likes of us, of a very special sort.

A book that has profoundly influenced my views on race relations has the title *Slave Religion*, written by the Princeton African-American historian Albert Raboteau. At one point in that book, Raboteau shows how the Christian slaves of the Old South typically had a deep reverence for the Bible, so much so that even those who did not know how to read nonetheless found ways to make the Bible a central focus of their devotional lives.

One of the stories Raboteau tells is about a young illiterate slave woman, a nursemaid to her master's family, who enlisted the white children to teach her how to recognize the word "Jesus." Having gained possession of a Bible, she would regularly find a quiet place where she would turn the pages of the Bible, running her fingers up and down the pages until she found the name of Jesus.

I admire that young slave woman. I want her kind of simple love of her Lord and her deep conviction that what the Bible is all about is Jesus. For those of us who have passed, as Christians, through the disciplined thinking afforded by programs in higher education, we can't simply forget all that we have learned—the questions, the times of doubts, the wrestling with various challenges to our faith. In the end, though, we need to cultivate what some scholars have called the "second naiveté." This means, for me, that the slave woman had it right. In the end, the Bible is all about trusting and following Jesus, the One who loved us so much that He came to live and die for the likes of us, doing for us what we could never do for ourselves.

Oliver Wendall Holmes put it well when he said, "I would not give a fig for the simplicity this side of complexity, but I would give my life for the simplicity that is on the other side of complexity." So here is a simple statement that I hope you can embrace on the other side of complexity as a profound expression of the second naiveté: when all is said and done, it is all about Jesus. That is what this school is all about in the final analysis—promoting the cause of Christ's Kingdom so that He, the Heaven-sent Messiah of God, might have preeminence in all things.

So my charge to you today is simply this: *be faithful to Jesus.* And do so with courage and unwavering commitment.

A few years ago around this time, the Jesuit magazine, *America*, asked various people what they would say if they were giving a commencement address. The Benedictine nun, Sister Joan Chittister, responded by saying that she would tell this story:

> Once upon a time, a warlord rampaged through the countryside, ravaging, and killing as he went. Word spread quickly from village to village, and the peasants fled for their lives. As he strode into the last of the villages, the warlord said with a smirk, "The village is empty, I presume?"
>
> "Well, yes, my Lord," his lieutenant answered. "Except, that is, for one monastic nun, a woman who refuses to leave." The warlord was furious. "Bring her to me immediately," he roared. So they

8 SERIOUS DREAMS

dragged the elderly monastic to the square. "Do you not know who I am?" the warlord shrieked. "I am he who can run you through with a sword without even batting an eye!" "And do you not know who I am?" the old monastic said, looking him straight in the eye. "I am she who can let you run me through with a sword—without even batting an eye."

That is the kind of courage we need from you in today's world where there is much to challenge us and many wonderful opportunities for service if we are willing to take them up with courage. But it isn't just about courage. The kind of courage we Christians need to cultivate has to be intimately linked to hope for the future.

And we do look forward to a glorious future. There is a greater commencement that is coming, and when we get to that commencement, we will wear robes again—not our academic robes at that commencement, but the pure robes of the righteousness of Jesus Christ.

Here is how the writer of the Book of Revelation describes that commencement:

> After this I looked, and there was a great multitude that no one could count, from every nation, from all tribes and peoples and languages, standing before the throne and before the Lamb, robed in white, with palm branches in their hands. They cried out in a loud voice, saying, "Salvation belongs to our God who is seated on the throne, and to the Lamb!" (Rev. 7:9–10)

That is where we are headed if we are followers of Jesus. So be faithful—live with courage and hope in obedience to the cause of the Gospel. And then we will see each other there at the more glorious commencement that is coming! Until then, God bless you all.

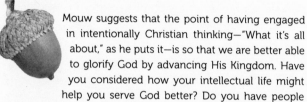

Mouw suggests that the point of having engaged in intentionally Christian thinking—"What it's all about," as he puts it—is so that we are better able to glorify God by advancing His Kingdom. Have you considered how your intellectual life might help you serve God better? Do you have people around you with whom to talk about the life of the mind?

What steps can you take to ensure that your intellectual life stays sharp and useful for God's sake? Be sure to finish this book, and make reading a regular spiritual discipline as you deepen your own discipleship and calling in the world.

. . . .

Richard J. Mouw is the former President of Fuller Theological Seminary in Pasadena, CA, where he now is the Professor of Faith and Public Life in the School of Theology. He transitioned from his undergraduate years at Houghton College, eventually earning a PhD from the University of Chicago. He is recognized as a renowned Christian leader and author of numerous books, including *Abraham Kuyper: A Short and Personal Introduction, Uncommon Decency: Christian Civility in an Uncivil World,* and *When the Kings Come Marching In: Isaiah and the New Jerusalem.*

YOU NEED
TWO EYES

NICHOLAS WOLTERSTORFF

DELIVERED AT
CALVIN COLLEGE
GRAND RAPIDS, MICHIGAN

I tell you a true story. Some years back, when I was doing some teaching at the Free University of Amsterdam, my wife and I had a discussion with an obstetrician on the academic staff of the university hospital. The question arose of how he taught prospective nurses to deal with mothers whose babies were stillborn or died shortly after birth. "I tell them," he said, "that when you go into the room, you need two eyes. With one eye you have to check the I.V.; with the other, you must cry. I tell them one eye is not enough. You need two eyes."

Everything I want to say to you is contained within that brief story. I was left in no doubt that my speech had to be short. Since the story makes my point, nothing much would be lost if I sat down right now. My guess is that it wasn't meant to be *that* short, however, so I'll say a bit more.

When you walk and drive around this campus, you see banners attached to the light poles with the motto "Minds in the Making." That refers to the first eye, the one that checks the I.V. It's the eye of the mind—the eye of knowledge and discernment. Every college and university is in the business of trying to see to it that its students know more when they leave than when they arrived. So those who devised this motto for Calvin College—"Minds in the Making"—must have had something else in mind than just knowing more. They must have believed that there is more to the mind that the college seeks to nourish in its students than mere increase in knowledge.

What might that "more" be? What is the mind that this school has sought to nourish in you? What is the mind that for generations the college has sought to nourish in its students? In my travels, every now and then I come across somebody about whom I say to myself, "He thinks like a Calvin grad, she thinks like a Calvin grad." Will I say that about you if I meet you ten years hence? If I do, what will I mean?

At a minimum, the mind that Calvin College has sought to nourish in you is the mind of competence. You know how to use the English language properly, even skillfully, and perhaps another language as well. You are well-trained in the skills of your future occupation. People can count on you to do things right and do them well. You know how to check the I.V. and how to correct it when something goes wrong.

But that's only the minimum. The person who thinks like a Calvin grad isn't just good at doing things the way things are done. She asks questions. She asks why things are being done this way. Why is it important that they be done this way? Why is it important that these things be done at all? In doing things this way, what assumptions are being made? Are those assumptions correct? What are the moral implications of doing things this way? How does doing things this way serve God's cause of justice and sha-lom? Is there integrity in doing things this way, or do you have to sell your soul to the devil? Can this way of doing things stand the light of day?

When I come across a person who thinks like this, I feel that I have found a soulmate.

This person has the sort of mind that I tried to nourish when I was a professor here. This person has the mind of a Calvin College grad. He may not be a Calvin grad; but if he is, I feel deep pride in this institution to which I devoted so many years of my life. This, I hope and believe, is the mind Calvin is referring to when it speaks of "Minds in the Making."

The best term I have for this way of thinking is critical engagement. You engage the world of nursing, of business, of law, of art, of medicine, of education, of politics, of recre-ation, whatever; you don't pull out, not unless integrity re-quires you to do so, as it sometimes does. But you engage it with critical discernment; you don't just run with the crowd. You say no when no must be said, and also, let me add im-mediately, yes when yes is to be said.

Be forewarned that critical engagement is likely to get

you into trouble; it's not a recipe for popularity at the office. People don't like having somebody around asking whether their customary ways of doing things are worthwhile, whether they are important, whether they have integrity, whether they serve God's cause of justice and shalom.

That was the first eye, the eye of the mind, the eye of knowledge and discernment. Now for the second eye, the eye of the heart, the eye that weeps. It may have occurred to you that you don't need good eyesight to have the eye of knowledge and discernment—you don't need eyesight at all, literally speaking. That's even truer for the second eye; in fact, it's probably easier for the blind person to have the eye of the heart than it is for the rest of us. We all recognize the need for the eye of knowledge and discernment. You yourself may not have described it in quite the way I did, but it's easy to see its importance in this knowledge-saturated world of ours. The need for the second eye is less obvious, and colleges and universities are much less good at nourishing it.

What good does a crying eye do? What good does it do the mother? What good does it do the nurse? What good does it do anybody? Why not stifle the cry and get on with knowledge and discernment? Why the eye of the heart?

The nurse weeps because the mother weeps. And the mother weeps because she loved her child. It was right that she loved her child for her child was a creature of great worth, a creature of God's own making meant to flourish until full of years, and a creature of Christ's own redeeming. Now the child is gone. The mother's weeping is the pained recognition that this is not how God meant things to be. It is her pained recognition of the fallenness of our world. Things have gone awry in God's world which, of course, is why God has committed Himself to redeeming it.

The nurse weeps for the same reason the mother weeps. "Weep with those who weep," said Paul to the Christians in Rome, to which he added, let me emphasize, "Rejoice with those who rejoice." The obstetrician that my wife and I talked with surely did not mean that if all goes well in childbirth, the nurse needs only the eye of knowledge.

Do you begin to see why you need the second eye? It's with the second eye that the pain of the world and the hope for a new day enters your heart. "Blessed are those who mourn," said Jesus. He was not blessing those who go around moping. He was blessing those who discern all the ways in which life in this world falls short of justice and shalom who then go on to say, "This must not be," and who struggle to change things when they see the chance of doing so. The mourners are discontented visionaries. They will be comforted, says Jesus.

I hope I have not given you the impression that the eye of the heart is relevant only to such professions as nursing and medicine. It's not. Every occupation and every profession touches human beings. Every occupation and every profession either advances justice and shalom or hinders it.

Some of you will be going into business. For that, you need two eyes. With one eye, you have to check accounts receivable and accounts payable, overhead and profit margins, payroll and insurance costs. With the other, you have to attend to your employees—are they receiving just reward for their labor, and can they find fulfillment in their work? And you have to think of your clients—do the products or services that you provide enhance their lives rather than diminish or debase them? One eye is not enough.

Some of you will be going into law. For that, you need two eyes. With one eye, you have to check the law books, dig out precedents, keep up with the courts, figure out what's best for your clients and fair to their adversaries. With the other, you have to discern and share in the pain and grief that almost always lie just below the surface of court proceedings and legal briefs. One eye is not enough.

Some of you will be going into teaching. For that, you need two eyes. With one you have to make lesson plans and read student papers, keep up with theories of reading and developments in math. With the other, you have to discern and feel the tender hearts of the students with whom you are dealing. One eye is not enough.

Some of you will be going into politics. For that, you need two eyes. With one eye, you have to figure out the intricate details of what justice and prosperity for all require in the present situation, both at home and abroad—not what keeping your own party in power requires, not what flexing your nation's muscles requires, but what justice and prosperity for all require. With the other eye, you have to weep with those who are abused, wronged, killed, and demeaned by all that goes wrong in politics. One eye is not enough.

Graduates, in whatever walk of life you find yourself, you will need two eyes. Whatever your walk, you will need knowledge and discernment, critical engagement. And whatever your walk, you will need compassion.

You will be touching the lives of human beings, creatures with minds like yours and hearts like yours, minds that seek understanding, hearts that suffer and rejoice. They are kinsfolk, creatures whose differences from you fade away before the fact that the Creator of the universe and Restorer of all that is fallen is mirrored in them and you alike. Do not be so focused on knowledge that you neglect compassion; do not be so overcome by compassion that you neglect knowledge.

The eye of the mind without the eye of the heart is heartless competence. The eye of the heart without the eye of the mind is mindless empathy. You need both eyes, both the eye of the mind and the eye of the heart, both the eye of discernment and the eye of compassion—one eye to check the I.V., the other to weep with those who weep and rejoice with those who rejoice.

One eye is not enough.

You need two eyes.

Wolterstorff says that we "need two eyes." One eye is for competence and good ideas, and the other is for empathy and compassion. Have you ever pondered how God wants us to have both capacities? In your life these days, which is your greatest strength? Which might you need to develop more? What steps might you take to pursue sharpening the vision of both of your eyes? Put another way, how can you develop both your mind and your heart?

Nicholas Wolterstorff is a highly respected philosopher, author of dozens of books, and currently serves as a Senior Fellow of the Institute for Advanced Study in Culture at the University of Virginia. His undergraduate years were spent in the early 1950s in Grand Rapids, MI where he studied at Calvin College. His PhD is from Harvard, and he holds an honorary doctorate from the Frije Universiteit, (Amsterdam) where he has been a visiting professor. He is a professor emeritus of Yale University and has also taught at Princeton, Oxford, Notre Dame and other prominent universities. He is a Fellow of the American Academy of Arts and Sciences. His memoir about becoming a scholar who sees with "two eyes" is called *Journey Toward Justice: Personal Encounters in the Global South.*

REJOICING
YOUR
COMMUNITY

AMY L. SHERMAN

DELIVERED AT
MALONE UNIVERSITY
CANTON, OHIO

I cannot honestly say that I remember *exactly* what I was thinking when I was sitting at my own college graduation, though I suspect I was hoping both that the speaker would be relatively brief and that I wouldn't trip on my way up to the stage to get my diploma. One of those two wishes came true that day—but I won't tell you which one.

I'd like to talk with you today about the short text you heard read from Proverbs 11:10. I chose it because I think it reflects very well the mission of this institution and offers to each of you graduates a challenging, robust, and joyful vision of what can come next in life for you.

Proverbs 11:10 says, "When the righteous prosper, the

city rejoices."

My favorite preacher, Tim Keller, has noted that this verse should seem somewhat counter-intuitive to us at first glance. After all, it says that there is a city, and in this city, there is one people group that is prospering. They enjoy great blessing—they have assets, power, opportunities, position, wealth, and talent. They are prospering, flourishing in every way. And the verse says that as this group prospers, *everyone* is happy about it. The whole city rejoices over it.

Now, that is counter-intuitive. Can't you easily imagine a more plausible scenario marked by jealousy and resentment? Isn't it more likely the people at the bottom of the city would be saying, "Here we go again, the rich just keep getting richer," rather than singing hallelujah over the increasing fortunes of the people at the top?

What makes the verse sensible is that the people who are prospering are "the righteous." The Hebrew word there is *tsaddiqim*. The *tsaddiqim*, the righteous, are defined as those who are so in love with God and His Kingdom that they steward everything they have been given—their assets, their social position, their vocational skills, their power, their gifts, their prosperity—not for self-enrichment, not for the purpose of self-aggrandizement, but for the *common good*. They steward all the dimensions of their prosperity for the purposes of shalom, for the purposes of advancing God's justice and goodness. And when the people at the top of the city—the people with influence and opportunities and talents and power—act like this, then of course the whole city rejoices. The people at the bottom rejoice *because they benefit.* By the way the *tsaddiqim* steward their gifts, they make life better for everyone.

"When the righteous prosper, the city rejoices."

Now, the word "rejoice" in this little verse is also very important. It's a unique term, used only one other time in the Old Testament. It has almost military connotations in how it denotes the ecstatic rejoicing and celebrating that a small people do when they achieve an unlikely victory against their enemies. It describes the exultation that people express when they have been delivered from the hand of their oppressors.

So, "rejoice" here is a big, robust word. This is deep, passionate rejoicing—not the rejoicing of a birthday party but VE-Day rejoicing, dancing in the streets of Paris rejoicing, the "war is over and we won" rejoicing!

By this we realize that the righteous, the *tsaddiqim*, in their prospering are making a very significant, noticeable impact on their city—for only this could prompt such extreme rejoicing. They are stewarding their gifts and talents in ways that are bringing about such deep, substantial, positive transformation in the city that the people are going wild with gladness and gratitude. Clearly, this is *not* a case of the righteous taking their used clothes over to the Salvation Army Thrift Store and the poor people of the city finding them there and being so happy to get a $200 dress for five bucks. No, this is the righteous advancing justice and shalom in their community in such a way that the people at the bottom stop being oppressed and start having real opportunity; where everyone is starting to experience more safety, more wholeness, more hope, more peace, more community.

Indeed, the profound rejoicing that is happening in the city when the righteous prosper *is a result of nothing less than foretastes of the Kingdom of God coming into reality in the city.* This kind of rejoicing occurs as the curse is pushed back and the virtues of the Kingdom are pushed in. When that happens, then the whole city dances and rejoices with abandon.

"When the righteous prosper, the city rejoices."

Graduates, I propose to you today that you *are* the prospering. Now I realize that at just this moment, you probably don't feel really powerful or prosperous. But just because you are not Bill Gates, and even though you have school loans to pay off, and even though you may fear you won't get a good job right away in this economy, you *are* the prosperous. Measured against the standards of life of many people in this nation and most people in this world, relative to those billions in poverty without occupational choice, without education, *you are the prospering*—as I am and the rest of your elders here. But the education you have received at Malone University was not primarily about enabling you to be the prospering, although I believe it has and will enable just that. No, the education you received here was about enabling you to be the *tsaddiqim*. You have been honing your God-given gifts and opportunities here for the purpose of service, for powerful service in this world, for the purpose of rejoicing your neighborhood, your community, your world.

One key element of being the *tsaddiqim* of God is stewarding that aspect of prosperity that is your vocational talent, power, and choice. And in this matter of vocational stewardship, many of the Malone alumni who have walked this stage before you have shown wonderful creativity and intentionality. I hope you will make it your aim to imitate such imagination and deliberateness.

Consider Ignatios Meimaris, class of 1974. He and his wife Nena moved to Greece roughly a decade ago to create the Interbalkan Institute for Educational and Economic Development. In the midst of the economic sorrows of Greece, this Christ-loving couple is bringing biblically-based business training to men and women who need new hope and are finding it through new enterprises.

Or consider a younger alumnus—Brandon Delise from the class of 2010. He's putting his degree in Community Health Education to work as he serves in the Peace Corps in the small African nation of Lesotho.

But you don't have to move across the globe to honor God and advance His Kingdom. You can do it right here in this city. Consider the work of Lori Jones Stokes who got her graduate management degree here at Malone in 2001. She has put her training to work right here in Akron-Canton helping to ensure justice and equity in critical public services. She was the City of Canton's fair housing manager for some years and now serves as the Equal Opportunity Employment Officer for the Akron Metro Regional Transit Authority.

Or consider Yvonne Brake, class of 1998, who for nearly 24 years has allowed God to use her talents to coach homeless women at the Haven of Rest mission to find new life. Or Dr. Ronald Crock, Malone class of 1988, who, as the director of the hospice program here at Mercy Medical Center in Canton, is bringing comfort and dignity to those at the end of their lives.

Chemists and management experts and business majors and teachers—Malone graduates of all types. As I look out at your beautiful faces, I know I'm seeing future pharmacists and educators, social workers and artists, engineers and linguists, physical therapists and accountants, nurses and political scientists, computer programmers and graphic designers, and ... you fill in the blank.

Many diverse callings, many diverse vocations—but the common thread is that the purpose of all of them is *service*. The alumni I've mentioned are stewarding their vocational power to advance foretastes of the Kingdom—foretastes of flourishing, of hope, of joy, of justice, of wholeness. They are deploying their gifts for the common good. They are living as the *tsaddiqim*.

Living this way has required intentionality. It has required faithfulness. Living this way requires creativity and imagination and risk and prayer and perseverance. For you see, it is frighteningly possible to be the prospering without being the *tsaddiqim*.

It is possible to be the prospering without being the *tsaddiqim* because of at least two great temptations.

One is a temptation from our secular culture. It is

the temptation of coming to believe that richness of having leads to richness of being, rather than the other way around. It is the danger of giving far too much weight to the material over the spiritual.

The second is a temptation from within some quarters of our religious subculture. It is the temptation of believing that the spiritual is *all* that matters, that our vocational lives here on this earth really don't count that much since, eventually, this world is simply going to burn up. When saving souls and getting a ticket to Heaven are all that really matter, then we will not rigorously pursue the question of how to steward our talents for the betterment of life on this earth—for the feeding of the hungry, the releasing of the oppressed, the care of the environment, and the nurturing of a people of shalom. If it's all going to burn up, then our vocations become merely our jobs, a means to make money, to live the comfortable American dream while we count on Jesus to get us into Heaven when our souls "fly away."

Thankfully, in your college years here, you have received grounding in a much more fully-orbed Christian world-and-life view, packed with truths, which can help you resist both these temptations.

I pray that the Spirit of Christ would work in you powerfully to help you continue to live by what Malone University has called its "foundational principles"—that is, a commitment to promote justice, civic responsibility, peace, and reconciliation, and through outreach, evangelism, and service, to witness to the love and grace of Christ.

May He enable you to live, not merely as the prospering, but as the *tsaddiqim*.

Sherman explained both the Biblical notion of caring for the common good as well as the Proverb that promises that the watching community will rejoice when the righteous prosper. Have you ever thought about your own professional success being so deeply connected to the needs of your community? Have you considered how your career or calling actually helps to serve others?

What can you do to deepen your awareness of how your work can help the world flourish and find ways to connect your vocation to the common good? Is there someone you admire with whom you could talk and pray about these things?

. . . .

Amy L. Sherman is a Senior Fellow at the Sagamore Institute for Policy Research and is author of several books, including the important *Kingdom Calling: Vocational Stewardship for the Common Good.* She transitioned from her years of undergraduate study at Messiah College to work at a Washington, DC think tank, then headed to the University of Virginia to complete her PhD. She stayed in beautiful Charlottesville, started and ran an urban ministry there for several years, and now serves as a "minister to ministries" around the country as they seek to bring flourishing to their communities.

THE MEMORY
IN THE SEED

CLAUDIA BEVERSLUIS

DELIVERED AT
CALVIN COLLEGE
GRAND RAPIDS, MICHIGAN

"Be kind. Dream big. Remember history. Embrace failure. Never give up." There, I have just given you all the advice that National Public Radio said is in the typical commencement speech. The trouble is—trouble more for you than for me—I have so much more to say.

Here is one thing I want to say: This is quite a view, right here in front of me. You are beautiful together. Congratulations.

And I don't just mean you 891 graduates. I mean this community that surrounds you. All these folks who have been working for you, supporting you, challenging you, paying for you, wanting you to graduate.

It is so great to see you all here.

For most of the past 8 years, I have had the privilege of welcoming new students at the opening convocation in the fall. If you came in as a first year student, you sat in these same chairs. We try to do that so you can imagine this day, imagine graduation. When we say that—that we are imagining your future—students laugh a little, almost like they can't think that this will actually happen to them. But here you are, you have learned and grown a lot, and it is happening!

You learned a new Calvin College vocabulary too, one that has taken on levels of meaning and complexity throughout your time here.

I used to think it would be fun to hand out Bingo cards at the beginning of the academic year. We would all carry around cards and fill them up as we heard the words—vocation, Creation/Fall/Redemption, virtues, worldview, Kingdom, promptly and sincerely, community—we could go on and on, couldn't we?

And then, when we heard someone call out BINGO in the middle of a class or a speech, it wouldn't be because we shared friends or acquaintances. Rather, it would be because we knew we shared a common vocabulary, a common inheritance, a way of seeing the world. We would know we shared a past.

A few years ago, I gave a talk to faculty at the beginning of a school year. I was talking about some of the real tragedies in the world and why we should bother working in a college in light of all that. This is what I said:

> *What pulls us back to our work, and what calls us to this place is the conviction that through our work together here, we are in fact praying for the world— we are sending people out to many places, to serve and explore and lead and follow . . . and the world needs these students.*
>
> *When, this year, we pray together for the needs of the world, know that God is answering our prayers, partly through the students who are arriving here on campus.*

Well, you arrived and you learned. And now, God is ready to answer our prayers for the world—and your prayers for the world—through you.

Maybe that feels like a burden, not just a sweet bit of advice.

But here is the thing, graduates: the world does need who you are and what you bring.

Every time I am privileged to attend your music and theater performances, see the heart you bring to your athletic victories and your defeats, watch you model honesty and care as you tell your stories in the student paper, see your care for stewardship in your engineering solutions and environmental projects, listen to the careful thinking and delight in scholarship and research projects, watch you care for one another, see you lead in places all over campus, watch you make community together, and hear your reflections on this afternoon, I am more convinced than ever that you will be a blessing to the world.

More and more, the world needs people whose mission is to make God and God's good news believable to others— not just through their words, but through the daily ways they live together.

How do you live in the world with the kind of *depth* and *justice* and *wholeheartedness* that our college's mission statement calls for?

Here is one tiny part of that answer: you find your identity in a long view of time. You live with a memory of the past and a vision of the future.

There is an image from a poem by Wendell Berry that never left my mind as I was thinking about this day because it captures how communities take the past into the future.

This is from a poem about a funeral, not a commencement. But it seemed a fitting way to think about what is ending here and what is beginning.

Berry compares us—what we carry with us, what we know, who we are—to seeds. Seeds have a past, seeds carry memory into a new life. They carry something of the history of how they were made. And then, seeds can take a shared history into a scattered, dispersed future.

Listen:

But our memory of ourselves, hard earned,
is one of the land's seeds, as a seed
is the memory of the life of its kind in its place,
to pass on into life the knowledge
of what has died. What we owe the future
is not a new start, for we can only begin

with what has happened. We owe the future
the past, the long knowledge
that is the potency of time to come . . .
The community of knowing in common is the seed
of our life in this place. . .
—Wendell Berry, "At a Country Funeral"

You have been a part of a community here. It has grown and flowered in some beautiful and some thorny ways while you were here. This community has shared joys and sorrows, victories and humiliations. We have memories hard earned.

Through our communal life, you have inherited an intellectual and spiritual legacy. We have shared a way of looking at things. We can laugh a bit at our common vocabulary because we have shared a way of speaking about the world.

We have shared theological shorthand—for example, the CFR, "Creation/Fall/Redemption" thing. We have shared our understanding of God's vast, incredible Creation, the scary strength of the Fall, our amazing Redemption, our future—all in grace. I trust that this language has grown in complexity and depth over your time here. But now, you can think of it this way—CFR becomes DNA, memory in the seed.

We have participated in and been shaped by what Wendell Berry calls a community of knowing in common. Sometimes willingly. Sometimes more reluctantly.

This immediate community—this particular version of

it—is coming to an end. Today is harvest day.

But you take this inheritance with you. All along, the beauty in what we have been seeing, the fruitfulness in you and in the community, has also been about growing the seeds that you now have the opportunity to plant in new places.

There is precious memory in that seed that can bring into future new life that which is ending today. We need you to pass it on.

Let me remind you of a few things about this seed that you take with you.

First, this seed has a past. This past is global, and it has grown plants that are strong and beautiful. Part of what this education has been about is giving you memories of our global heritage.

You have seen or heard about communities around the world with a shared history and passion—educators in Indonesia, missionary communities from Korea, human rights workers in South Africa, brave justice advocates in Honduras, faithful resistors in Hungary, courageous pastors in Egypt, social workers in Liberia, and in so many other places.

Last fall I was in Indonesia, in a room full of 500 educators, mostly from Indonesian universities. And there, projected up in front of them all, in this faraway land, was a quote from a former Calvin College professor, Gordon Spykman:

It can be said that nothing matters but the Kingdom,
but because of the Kingdom, everything matters.

And it reminded me of how a planted seed can grow in

beautiful new ways. Around the world, we share a past.

What we have tried to give you is what has been given to us over many generations. It is a hardy, world-wide plant with deep roots, and it survives through tough times because it has been tested in tough times.

Many of us have seen concrete cracked and walls broken down because of what grew from a single feisty seed with deep roots.

This is your inheritance.

Second, this seed is about the future. We plant seeds in anticipation of future blessing.

What is the "long knowledge" that we know in common? What is the conviction about the future that we most need you to pass on into new life?

This: the conviction that Jesus Christ, who redeemed us, will be with us to the end and will bring to life a new Heaven and new Earth. This seed, this legacy, what you take with you now, contains a vision of this new Heaven and new Earth.

We have tried to envision together this future flourishing, and then we have tried to live, in some small way, into it:

Cities and countrysides that are healthy.
Nations without war.
Labor, craft, art, with joy and without exploitation.
Young women and men, growing up without fear,
    illness, death, kidnapping.
Worshiping multitudes, from every tribe and nation.
Beauty, strength.

I hope that much of your education was about giving you this kind of imagination. I hope that no matter where you go from here, you hang on to this vision. Pass on this imagination, this conviction about the full, whole, healed, redeemed future. Plant this seed.

Finally, this seed, this way of knowing in common, gives us a task. Between past and future, we have a job to do.

What do we do tomorrow, especially when it seems that there is no clear road map? What do you do?

Just start by finding one small place to plant a seed.

Every time your gut aches and your heart breaks because of the wounds in the world, because of the vastness of injustice, and you feel the pain of it, especially for and with others, you are planting a seed. Find a place to share the pain.

Every time you stand with astonishment and awe at the gifts God has given to us and share your amazement and gratitude in some way, you are planting a seed. Find a place to be astonished and grateful.

Every time you gravitate toward a place where you recognize Christ's redemptive work, and you join the work, in some small part of God's world, you are planting a seed.

Every time you gather together and make God a little more believable to others, a little more visible because of how you worship, work, and love, you are an agent of renewal because you are planting seeds.

Graduates, nothing done in the name of Jesus Christ, no seed planted in God's name, is wasted.

A seed is not designed to sit on a shelf in a little Lucite

case next to your diploma and tassel. It becomes a gift, your gift to the future, only when it is planted.

There is a lot of comfort in this, even when you have no idea what tomorrow will bring you. Because, if we offer our everyday lives to the God who made us and loves us, roots will grow, and they will yield fruit in due season. God will take care of the growth.

And when you sit in the 50-year alumni section, up there behind your grandchildren, you too will be able to testify to how God took this seed and grew it, gave it deep roots and maybe some unexpected thorns, perhaps cracked a few walls or foundations, and blessed the world—and then created new generations of seeds to be planted again and again.

Today we celebrate harvest and planting, planting and harvest, Christ's renewing work through you and in you. The world needs you. It needs what you are carrying.

Congratulations, and God bless you.

Beversluis used a Wendell Berry poem to remind us that we are to sow seeds inspired by our best memories of what we learned during our college years. Reflect on your own college years (or those most formative in recent years), and name some things that you learned that might be of value as you "pay it forward" and sow seeds of hope for the world.

Read "At a Country Funeral" again, and consider what it may mean that we "owe the future the past." Perhaps write a journal entry about it, or share your ruminations with a friend.

Claudia Beversluis delivered this commencement speech after serving for fifteen years in higher education administration as both a Dean and then the Provost of Calvin College, Grand Rapids, MI where she now serves as a Professor of Psychology. She made her transition out of undergraduate study from Calvin College, earned a PhD in clinical psychology from Loyola University of Chicago, and has served as a clinical psychologist, minister of congregational life, and professor. Her current interests are in psychology and justice, psychology and religion, and international Christian higher education. She recently spent time in India and Hong Kong working on faculty development and launching a Christian college. It was her moving graduation day speech that first inspired this collection.

COMMON
GRACE
FOR THE
COMMON
GOOD

STEVEN GARBER

DELIVERED AT
COVENANT SEMINARY
ST. LOUIS, MISSOURI

I suppose I was a favorite of the librarians in my hometown. Week by week, I would come in, see what was on the shelf, and bring several books home. My favorites were of the frontiersmen who made their way across America, crossing the great Mississippi and going up the long Missouri, over the Rockies and into the great beyond, the West, in all its majesty and mystery.

But if the biographies of Jim Bridger and Kit Carson captured me, there was another stream of story that I loved too. These were the stories of the French Revolution, full of sword-fighting and adventure, of right vs. wrong, of hope vs. heartache—*Scaramouche,* and *The Scarlett Pimpernel,* and *A Tale of Two Cities.* I loved them, far away as they were from my growing up years in California.

A few weeks ago, my wife, Meg, and I were in Paris with some of our children and grandchildren. We rented a flat in the neighborhood long-named the Bastille. From the windows of our flat, we could see the unholy ground itself—once home to that which was most hated by the French people, so much so that the attack on the Bastille was their first act when they finally rose up against their king and queen. Two hundred years later, it is home to the great tower that Napoleon built so as to remember to remember. In every way, it is a sober memory, full of violence just as it was on both sides of the revolution.

The Bastille is a half hour walk to Notre Dame, and on our first night there we walked through the ancient streets, taking it all in. And then, wonder of wonders, surprise of surprises, we turned around on a bridge over the Seine and saw a gloriously full moon! It was just about as good as it gets, so very beautiful.

But not all nights in Paris have been beautiful which brings us back to swordfights and *Scaramouche, The Scarlet Pimpernel,* and the storming of the Bastille, the icon of indifference of the French aristocracy with the cup of the people's anger finally overflowing in 1790.

That tells the tale too soon, though. Five hundred years earlier, another King Louis reigned over France. Though with our modern sensibilities, we may shake our heads at some of his decisions—for example, building a chapel to honor his most prized relic of faith, the crown of thorns—

he is remembered as the most devout of French kings, being sainted 35 years after his death. Yes, Sainte Louis.

In hope, King Louis built a beautiful chapel, an amazingly magnificent chapel. We call it Sainte Chapelle, with its 15 windows, each one 50 feet high. The Story of all stories is told, artfully and dramatically, the Narrative of all narratives; yes, the meta-narrative, the Biblical story from creation to consummation, of the way the world ought to be, the way the world is, the way the world can be, and the way the world someday will be. It is the story that Augustine told 1000 years earlier, of *posse peccare, posse non peccare,* of who we are and what we are as sons of Adam and daughters of Eve, making our way across time from creation to consummation with its promise of redemption as far as the curse is found. Here at Covenant Seminary in St. Louis, we know this as the history of redemption which Geerhardus Vos brought into the modern world in his magisterial text *Biblical Theology.*

Human being and lover of God that he was with long-ings that drove him like they do us, King Louis' questions are the perennial questions, the ones that human beings have always asked, are always trying to answer. And because of his own piety, he asked them in light of what he most deep-ly believed to be true. How will we live in the world? What will it mean to *live* in the world *under* the Word? That was the question of King Louis in his time, and, of course, it is the question for everyone in every time.

When it was built, Sainte Chapelle was situated within the grounds of the royal palace; centuries later, it is now the Palace of Justice, the chief court of France, completely surrounding the chapel, with *libertie, equalitie*, and *fraternitie* inscribed in stone over the main entrance. In fact, it almost seems architecturally unfair that the buildings are so close to each other, but they represent the pushing-and-shoving of a messy world where faith and life, Christian belief and the public square, butt up against each other.

A few hundred years later, the Louvre became the royal palace; and even later, Versailles was made the seat of the king and his queen. Tragically, for them and for the world, when Louis XV later pronounced himself a god and Sun King, it all eventually imploded. France fell in on itself, and the kings and queens lost their glory and their lives.

At this same time, during these centuries of social/ economical/political/ecclesiastical evolutions that some-times became revolutions across the English Channel and north into Scotland, the Reformation began, and Presbyterians began to protest over the same questions. How will we live in the world? What will it mean to *live* in the world *under* the Word?

Early on, in the days following Knox's preaching in St. Andrews, two brothers, James and Andrew Melville, gave an important speech to King James at his hunting palace in Scotland.

> *"There are two kings and two kingdoms in Scotland, your majesty."*

This was the first time in modern history that the divine right of the king was called into question. Looking back on this, we remember James more for his Bible than for this crucial moment in the long conversation about the Gospel and the world, the perennial sorting out of which coins belonged to which kings.

Readers of our world argue that this speech and the reformation it spawned had a great influence on the founding of America a century later with our own unique-in-history configuring of faith to life, of religious belief with the public square—namely, that there should be no establishment of religion for the sake of the free exercise of religion.

This is, of course, the history and heritage of the Presbyterian and Reformed traditions here in the United States which, over time, became Covenant Theological Seminary.

The ideas and issues that run through this short history are still wrangled over by every nation on the face of the earth today. The great tinderboxes of the twenty-first century are each their own story of faith and life, of worldviews with the world, grating, grinding, pushing and shoving. They are never cheap questions, and, therefore, there are never cheap answers. Think about them.

What does Jerusalem have to do with Athens?
Religious conviction with cultural power?
What is the relationship of religion to life?
The Gospel with life?
What is the relationship between the Christian vision of life and the world with how we live in the world?

Honest questions, each and every one, and each

requiring an honest answer. And for those with ears to hear, this reminds us of Francis Schaeffer and his long love for Covenant Theological Seminary. Honest questions and honest answers are the pedagogical threads that have run through my life making sense of my work as a teacher. The Institute here in Schaeffer's honor is an important memory of his vision and its influence on so many. Among many words that he loved, "presuppositions" stands out. He taught people to think *presuppositionally*, and he gave his life for the truth of the Gospel which he understood as the presupposition for a good life.

It is an important word as it reminds us to remember our deepest convictions, our pre-theoretic commitments. Like all human beings, like all institutions, we stand here on certain beliefs about the way the world is and ought to be.

If there is a presupposition upon which Covenant Seminary lives and moves and has its being, it is the reality of the covenant and the covenantal cosmos. That is the heart of your heritage as a seminary and tradition and the very core of what is most to be prized and therefore stewarded as you graduate and step into the vocations that you will have as you serve others.

Covenant is, of course, both a word and a doctrine. We speak meaningfully of an old and a new covenant, of a Noahic covenant, of a Mosaic covenant, even of the covenant becoming flesh in Jesus Christ. But I want to press into the word with you, insisting that it is also a word that gives life to human beings longing to belong to something some-where. In fact, it is a word that makes sense of our deepest

hopes as human beings. In its own remarkable way, it is
the answer to every question—at least, every question that
matters most.

Think with me about the rich, textured vision of "covenant"
that allows us a way of making sense of life in a modern-
becoming-postmodern world—full as it is of fragmentation
and anonymity, and, therefore, of indifference and irrespon-
sibility. These, in their own ways, are the heart-aching, tragic
faces of our cities and societies in the twenty-first century,
and we all feel their weight.

At the end of the day, we have no other universe to
live in than the covenantal cosmos of God—it is not a
"whatever" world, after all, because it cannot be so. We
may not prefer it or choose it or want it, but it is the world
that is really there because it is God's world, the covenantal
cosmos of God. Yes, this reality is the ground for our exist-
ence as human beings—the sons of Adam and daughters
of Eve that we are.

And yet, dear brothers and sisters, on this graduation
eve, to have mastered the theological vision is not enough.
We are called to the work of translation, of taking this
education into a pluralizing, secularizing, globalizing world
which is the world of St. Louis of Missouri and these United
States, of Europe and Asia and Africa and Latin America.
It is our world.

It is our world. And yet, in the now-but-not-yet of
our time in history, we live within two worlds—the
covenantal cosmos of God and the pluralizing, secularizing,

globalizing world of the twenty-first century. How do we hold them together with any kind of coherence? All of us live between both worlds; and in that, there is a tension for all of us. Sometimes it seems that we are stretched beyond what we can bear. And sometimes, sometimes we find ways to hold onto our integrity and still live with faith and hope and love. Please hear me clearly: more profoundly and pervasively than we could imagine, the theological education of Covenant Seminary takes place within the pressures and challenges of a pluralizing, secularizing, globalizing world.

Years ago, I came one summer to the faculty gathering of the seminary and offered the ideologies of both the prestigious magazine called *The Economist* and the farmer/writer Wendell Berry to the Covenant faculty. I was maintaining that, in their different ways, both were drawing on the reality of the covenant and the covenantal character of the cosmos—the one in the editorial vision of the magazine, in the very words that were used; the other in Berry's novels and essays and poems, never using the word but assuming it in everything he wrote. I was pressing this point: how do we take the idea of "covenant" and see that it makes sense of life for everyone everywhere? Even *The Economist* sees that. Do we? Even America's most serious essayist understands that. Do we?

I want tell you a story of my work with the Mars Corporation. Yes, they make M&Ms and much more. For almost 100 years, Mars has been making its presence known in the marketplaces of the world, selling nearly

$35 billion worth of products yearly. M&Ms, yes, but Dove Ice Cream bars too, Wrigley's Gum, Uncle Ben's Rice, and lots and lots of pet food. A family-owned company, Mars has long been committed to several principles—quality, efficiency, freedom, mutuality, and responsibility. In fact, they are committed to putting these principles into action in the push-and-shove of the global marketplace.

About eight years ago, I was drawn into a conversation with two executives who were tasked with a complex question—"How much money should we make?" It may seem a silly question in a Milton Friedman-shaped world. Why wouldn't you maximize profit? Why wouldn't you make the most money possible?

But if mutuality and responsibility are built into the corporate vision, into the institutional identity of the company, it changes the purposes and plans of business. If we are, in fact, honestly and actually bound by mutuality, then we see that we are in this together, all of us, everywhere. All the employees, all the supply-chain, everyone. And if responsibility is going to be honestly operative, then we have to see that our relationships with each other make us responsible for each other. Mutuality and responsibility feed on each other. They define each other.

And they do so because *life is covenantal.* And because life is covenantal, a more complex bottom line is required, one that honestly accounts for profit and people and the planet, all together.

I remember a day in the Mars headquarters setting forth this argument—we live in a covenantal cosmos, and that is why the words "mutuality" and "responsibility" make sense of business at its best, of the marketplace at its most meaningful. Not in abstraction, but in the metrics and spreadsheets, in the business plans and proposals that are the heart of the business anywhere and everywhere. The ultimate goal is not "Christian" M&Ms. In a pluralizing, secularizing, globalizing world, we are called to create signposts of what might be, of what could be, of what someday will be.

Ours is a work of translation, isn't it? It is a work of taking what is true and making it understandable to the wide world. If we have ears to hear, then when we hear mutuality and responsibility, we will hear "covenant."

Covenant is not only the name of a seminary but is even more so an idea that forms our deepest longings as human beings; it carries implications for families, for neighborhoods, for businesses and economies, for schools and schooling, for politics, for all the rest of life. We all want to belong, profoundly so, and "covenant" makes sense of that, especially of the mutuality and responsibility built into its very meaning.

For a long time, I have been asking this question. It is one for all of us tonight, especially for the graduates— can you sing songs shaped by the truest truths of the universe in language that the whole world can understand? I first began asking this of people in the music business— and it is their question, of course. But have you learned to do that in your years here with the vocation that is yours? Have you learned this vision of the God of the covenant

and of His covenantal cosmos so well that you can tell it
to the whole world? Are you graduating with the vision of
teaching others to do that in and through their vocations?

Asked a thousand ways in a thousand congregations,
it is our question as the people of God today. Can we?
Will we?

Will we see our stewardship of learning about God
and His world, about the history of redemption, about the
meaning of persons, about the nature of the human heart,
about the vision of the covenantal cosmos—will we see this
as a stewardship to the glory of God for the sake of the world?

Will you as preachers and teachers, pastors and coun-
selors, those trained to know much about the things that
matter most, take up this long story of God's work in the
world remembered so gloriously in the windows of Sainte
Chapelle and tell it in your own ways in your own lives?

Can you tell the story in ways that the butchers and
bakers and candlestick-makers, men and women in business, in law, in social service, in education, in farming, in
healthcare, at home, and in neighborhoods, will see their
work as translators of the Story of stories in and through
their own vocations, being and bringing common grace for
the common good?

We gather tonight here in Saint Louis to remember
to remember the vision of vocation that grows out of the
biblical story remembered in the windows built by Sainte
Louis which, strangely, wonderfully and providentially,
is the theological ground of institutional being here at

Covenant Seminary. We now step into history, into the wonderful and wounded, beautiful and broken world of the twenty-first century. That is what a graduation is, and we commission you this night for that purpose.

The ancient story is still true, even and especially so in the pluralizing, globalizing, and secularizing twenty-first century—true to the way the world always has been and always will be, the covenantal cosmos that it is.

May it be so, in and through your lives, ever more faithfully, ever more fully, as your educations form your vocations—to the glory of God, for the sake of the world.

Garber took us on a journey from Sainte Louis in France to St. Louis in Missouri. Besides the fact that his speech was delivered in St. Louis, he showed that people everywhere always ask the deepest of existential questions: Who are we? Where are we? What are we to do? Garber suggested the biblical view of the covenant as an essential aspect of any true answer to these profound questions. Why do you think he said that? What do you think he means by a "covenantal cosmos?"

What difference does it make for your worldview to have deeply biblical answers to the largest questions of your own identity and your place in the world? Think about ways to connect your most basic beliefs as a person of faith with your job and how your life is unfolding. Think of another person who might appreciate chatting about these sorts of things, and share with them what you are thinking about, especially regarding what Garber calls "visions of vocation."

Steven Garber is a teacher of many people in many places, and is the Principal of The Washington Institute, which is focused on the meaning of vocation for the common good. For many years on the faculty of the American Studies Program in Washington, DC, he has studied the intersection of popular culture with political culture. He is a consultant to businesses, foundations and educational institutions, including the Murdock Trust, the Wedgwood Circle, the Demdaco Corporation, Mars, Inc., and Praxis Labs. His most recent book is *Visions of Vocation: Common Grace for the Common Good*. A native of the great valleys of Colorado and California, he is married to Meg and they have five adult children whose lives have taken them all over the world.

THREE
CHEERS
FOR SONS &
DAUGHTERS
OF ISSACHAR

BYRON BORGER

DELIVERED AT
GENEVA COLLEGE
BEAVER FALLS, PENNSYLVANIA

The sons of Issachar are mentioned in 1 Chronicles 12:32. You may know the context:

In this chapter of the book which chronicles some of the stories in ancient Israel's history, a dramatic plot is underway to make young David the king. There already is a sitting king, so there will have to be a coup. The text lists those who are involved in this redemptive adventure, and they each seemed to have certain characteristics, things for which they were known. Some were particularly strong, some had spears, some prayed well; you get the picture: each was known for a quality which could be named, they had developed a reputation, a legacy. Several of the tribes are mentioned and then, almost in passing, it notes the sons of Issachar, and the reputation for which they were known. Do you recall it? Their legacy, what they would contribute to the work of God, is this: they "understood the times and knew what God's people should do."

That's it. They knew the times. And they knew a Godly response.

I think it is obvious that there are many cultural critics today, those who know a lot about how the world works. They are astute about what is going on in society and what makes things happen. They have an eye to discern the troubles in our society; they can name well the idols that function in our culture. On one hand, there are those who seem to understand the times.

On the other hand, there are those who know God, who seem to know the Scriptures, who are very pious and very spiritual. These folks are often very comfortable talking about their beliefs. They are clear about the gospel and they are joyful in their faith.

But this is the legacy of Issacharians: they have both qualities! They understand the times and they know what a Godly response might be. They understand the world and they understand a Biblically-faithful evaluation and response and perspective on the world. They have sophistication in their cultural awareness and insight about how God fits into it all, what God requires in these times.

That's a son or a daughter of Issachar. And they are rare to find.

As Steve Garber, himself a Geneva grad and author of *Visions of Vocation: Common Grace for the Common Good*, has put it, such Issacharians are skilled at "reading the world and reading the Word." Might that describe you?

Of course, mostly we read the world in *light of the Word*. That is a significant part of having a Christian worldview. That's what John Calvin meant went he described the Bible as a set of spectacles—eye-glasses. The Word is a "light before our path" and that means we don't so much stare into it, but allow it to light up everything we do in God's world. The Bible is like a miner's lamp—the light on our helmet that shines from over our head onto our work, illuminating what we're doing.

So, for years you've studied here, like miners, digging in to your little corner of the world, by the light of the Word.

And sometimes it works the other way around. We sometimes need to (with great care and awareness of how this can be risky) read the Word in light of the world. The stuff we've learned in our classes, and in our lives, cycles back and informs how we understand God, the Scriptures, and God's present work in the world.

As graduates—life-long learners, involved in the world, engaged in the Biblical story, taking up your calling to various careers and professions—you will be involved in this process of reading the Word and understanding the times for the rest of your days.

This is the amazing calling of sons and daughters of Issachar, who stand fully on the Word of God but also stand fully in God's world, studying it, caring for it, learning how to serve it, attending to the contours of the ordinances God has actually embedded in His creation. Jesus Christ made and upholds all aspects of the creation (it says so in Colossians 1) and therefore you have actually been studying His precious handiwork, opening yourselves up to discover wonder and wisdom in business administration, special education, cardiac science, reading, counseling, higher education and all the other fields that are explored here. Some of you are going to go on and study more, pursuing academia as a calling. Most of you will be engaged in continuing professional development in your career area. Remember: you are studying God's world, wherever you go, whatever you are learning.

You have spent time becoming equipped to be a son or daughter of Issachar, which is to say, a thoughtful and wise servant of Yahweh, the King of the Universe. You've studied hard and learned as much as you could about a certain corner of God's world. Now you are being commissioned to apply what you know to your chosen career and calling. You now get to live that out more fully, putting feet on the ideas that have grown here, sharing what you know with the watching world, and even advising others with insight from your own specialty area. Some of you may even end up, in time, like Daniel or Joseph, serving in important places in the pagan Empire. Let us hope that this is so, and that when you arrive at positions of influence, you can serve as discerning daughters and sons of Issachar.

God is working His purposes out in institutions and

workplaces and neighborhoods everywhere, and we are celebrating this day the work you've done which has prepared you to serve well within those disciplines and destinations.

Because you've studied, you have a better idea of what it looks like to be, as Jesus put it, salt, light, leaven, to be "doers of the Word" (James 1:22.) You've heard what it means (as the Hebrew prophet Jeremiah put it in his own culture of disarray) to "seek the peace of the city" and so you know a bit of how we can offer (in Calvin Seerveld's colorful phrase) "rainbows for the fallen world." I know you've heard these things here, and I pray that you will not forget them, these promises and challenges.

Most of you, I assume, were fine Christian people before you matriculated here. But I also believe, with the learning you've experienced here, the mentors you've found, the academic community you've been a part of, the papers you've written, the projects you've completed, the research you've done, the new ideas you've examined, you now have (as I've heard Richard Mouw put it) *more* to be Christian *with*.

Your time here has so grounded you in the drama of Scripture—God's true Story—that you have deeper capacities for faithful, Biblically-informed cultural discernment and what might even be called a prophetic imagination. You long to have the mind of Christ, and exhibit a humble passion to be a life-long learner.

You've learned some things that matter, you've developed some skills of cultural discernment, learned a healthy posture toward the world, absorbed some wisdom about what God thinks about your career, even what practices might be most fruitful as you serve as God's person in the marketplace and workforce. Whether you find yourself in a factory or lab or school or shop, in a cubicle or a studio, a high-rise office or an office in your home, you have been given a lot which you now get to apply.

Let's be honest. I don't know if this degree—completed now after a very long haul—will get you better wages or more earning potential right away. I really don't know if this degree will get you a better job.

And you wondering that, too.

But I hope you do know, deep in your bones, that you have taken up higher learning not just to get a better paying job, but because knowing things matters.

It matters greatly that you are now better thinkers, more aware of the world, better skilled at the art of considering Christianly. It matters to your own self-confidence and it matters—get this!—to your neighbors and our world.

Most people in our modern culture may not quite realize it at first, but your fruitful service for the common good will make the world a better place. Our neighbors are crying out for answers; our secular age is confused, at best, and longing for coherence and sanity and hope. Your refreshing approach to your callings and careers, your perspective which directs the way you work, and your lives lived well, will be signs of hope.

And, further, the Bible says that the world will actually glorify God if they see you doing good stuff (Matthew 5:16.) Your degree and the beneficial fruit it will bear, if you continue to be faithful, will cause the world to praise God. That's pretty exciting, isn't it? You help to elicit more worship for the Triune God of the universe, simply by doing good work. Our neighbors are better served, our culture may be renewed, and the great God of our Lord and Savior, gets more praise—through you!

That is why we are here today. To get you commissioned, so the world gets repaired and God gets glorified!

So, I am honored and excited to say "three cheers for you sons and daughters of Issachar!"

A CHEER FOR THE PAST Did you know that Geneva College was once a stop on the underground railroad, a part of the abolitionist movement? Leaders here in the past put it all on the line and risked their reputations and the institution's survival by doing the right thing, leading the way in social justice.

Geneva was one of the early colleges to grant degrees to women.

The famous Christian philosopher of culture, Francis Schaeffer, visited here from Switzerland in the early 1970s; this place was one of two locations where he gave impressive lectures which then were published and became the important book, *Art and the Bible.* Right here at Geneva!

Decades ago this college partnered with urban and black churches to start Centers for Urban Studies in Philadelphia and Pittsburgh. To see conservative, largely white institutions partner with people of color, using the resources and social capital of the college community for the sake of others is a glorious legacy.

You should remember those kinds of initiatives, those who took risks, and be proud and inspired.

There is an amazing heritage here, a story of innovative and culturally-relevant education, Biblically-faithful, but with a vision of wide-as-life discipleship and global service. You may not have chosen this school because of its legacy, but you are now a part of it. It is the same for anyone, at any institution. I offer a big cheer this day (and hope you do, too) for your college's good work in the past and for how that heritage has blessed the world, and for how you are now characters in the plot of that story. (In other words, stay in touch with your alumni office. And your favorite professors. And your best friends. This is a story you are a part of, not a chapter to merely leave behind.)

A CHEER FOR THE PRESENT In my work as a bookseller I am privileged to consult with professors and students to suggest books that will help them "think Christianly" about their own particular fields, and their professional development. I know there are on-going conversations here, as there are in many college settings, about what some call the "integration of faith and learning." I want to give a very loud cheer for this very contemporary aspect of Christians in higher education—one you have been a part of, and for which we honor you this day.

I would like to commend to you two Bible verses that will remind you that intellectual considerations must not become a thing of the past for you. I hope these texts capture your hearts and minds and shape your conversations as you leave this place, making your way into the wider world.

Colossians 2:8 This is a verse that is very important for young scholars—for any of us, really—and it expresses the idea that we are not to be hoodwinked by the ideologies around us. It says, specifically, "don't be taken captive..." by philosophies and theories and ideas that aren't of Christ. You see, this is an Issacharian kind of verse: as the somewhat similar Romans 12:2 puts it, we must not be squeezed into the mold of the world around us. This Colossians text is a defensive mandate, so to speak, a warning: be on guard, don't let them get to you, those with inappropriate and seductive theories about things. We must engage the ideas of the day, but we must be discerning about alluring voices, bad books, the assumptions and distorted values of popular films and TV shows, the dehumanizing attitudes driving many careers. "Don't be taken captive" and consequently be put to work for some other philosopher's agenda. It seems to me that Colossians 2:8 is a warning for anyone reading, thinking, advancing in the contemporary world, and we simply must take it to heart. Don't get sucked in to ways of seeing life, or thinking about the particulars in your own career, that are in conflict with what we know from the Biblical story. Don't be taken captive.

2 Corinthians 10:5 Ahh, now, this is the more positive way of saying it. Here, we are to "take every thought captive" for Christ. Notice the similarities? The Greek word in this phrase, usually translated "thought" actually means theories. That is, we are to take every theory about things—about your major, your academic field, your work, our society and its goals—captive for Christ, construing these ideas as God would want, putting those thoughts (distorted and pagan as they may be) to work to advance God's Kingdom. "Take every theory captive!" Again, this is an Issacharian verse, an essential habit of mind for those serious about integrating faith and learning, and learning with life.

According to these two texts we must not allow ourselves to be overly-influenced by unbiblical ideas and ideologies. Obviously, we cannot ignore the culture in which we live, so we must be engaged in the world of theories and philosophies but always engaged from a mature and faithful Christian frame of reference. We must struggle with the ideas debated in our culture (and the practices that emerge from them) being sure not to be taken captive by them, but in order to, as the text says, appropriate those ideas for God's Kingdom purposes.

Now that you are no longer in the classroom you must recommit yourself to these two tasks, from these two texts from God's Word. It just takes some work, wisely construing the ideas of our culture and framing them in light of what we know to be true, being discerning, as the sons and daughters of Issachar that you are.

You have learned in college to be a certain kind of critical thinker—one with a Bible in your hand, the common good of cultural shalom on your horizon, and a concern for the reputation of God Almighty in your heart.

You have learned much, and been encouraged to integrate what you are learning within your own Christian formation, to develop a Christ-like mind and heart and a passion to be faithful in the world, living well and doing good. One of your own professors here, Dr. Esther Meek, has written several books about "longing to know" and what it means to know things deeply and allowing what we know to actually shape us into responsible people. Oh my, what a great, great, life-long project, knowing things truly, and being responsible with what we know.

You have worked hard and been diligent in thinking about these things, in your own field, in your academic discipline, and you have learned to discern the principles God has embedded in the creation, even as you ponder your own vocation and calling and career. This is what I cheer for now, this very important academic work you've done, integrating faith and learning, studying God's creation, and engaging the life of the mind, taking ideas to heart and a sking what it means to be responsible with what you've studied and learned. And you've done this for the particular occupation or profession to which you believe God has called you. You have begun to think of your future jobs not merely as ways to pay your bills, but as holy callings, vocations.

It is the Geneva graduate, Steve Garber, who gave us a phrase that has captured the imagination of many: *vocation is integral, not incidental, to the mission of God.* That sounds like a good slogan for Issacharians and seriously Christian college graduates.

In other words, all this talk about a Christian worldview, a Biblically-shaped mind, a vision of creation healed, a faith-based view of vocation, and a spirituality of work aren't just things we say at graduation and it isn't just for a few of us. This is the good news of the gospel—God's Kingdom is coming ("on Earth as it is in heaven") and we get to be in on it! We are all called to enter the story of God's mission, and our sense of vocation is central to the role we get to play.

Dear friends, this is very exciting, and great, great news: Christ's rule can be woven into the fabric of every single part of our lives. It is not incidental, but integral.

Steve learned about the far-reaching implications of that word—integral—from his own years here at Geneva from a professor who has since died, but who left an amazing legacy at several colleges and campus ministry organizations—Dr. Peter J. Steen.

If you care today as a follower of Jesus about urban renewal or racial reconciliation, about climate change or the need for religious freedom, the influences of technology or the idols of the marketplace, about a Christian philosophy of sports or schooling or science, know that those questions and the struggle for deep conversations about the issues of the day are encouraged, even authorized among us. This is in part because of the influence of this integral and transforming vision that is in the DNA of Geneva College's Reformed tradition, which was underscored and worked out by Dr. Steen and his students, some of whom have taught you these past years and are sitting here among us today.

But yet, there is another part of this story. We must speak of the turmoils and tragedies of human sin, the inevitability of conflict, the frustrations of institutional stubbornness, and the difficulties of achieving lasting social reform. You see, it isn't easy being a son or daughter of Issachar.

So, I need to tell you this: it is likely that some of us here, so honored this wonderful, glad day, will face painful, maybe devastating conflict because of your faithfulness to the integral principles you've learned here. If you are in the vanguard of God's project relating faith in wise and redemptive ways to the worlds of business, medicine, science, higher education, in non-profits and the arts, in labs and in schools, in media and clinics and factories and corporations and law firms and real estate offices you will experience (I am sure of it) great joy and, I hope, much success. But I also know you must be prepared to suffer.

Issacharians are on a mission for God and they will often be on a collision course with trouble.

Maybe it is uncouth or bad manners to say this here in the middle of our happy celebrations, but there it is: Jesus said, "They hated me, they will hate you too." Unlike what most graduation speakers say, I need to tell you, beloved friends, it's not going to be easy.

Reformed Presbyterian Covenanters (like you here at Geneva) who are in the habit of Psalm singing know this well, since a third of the Psalms are laments and protests. Those dirges and laments are in our Book, they are our poems, and they give us words to say and ways to understand suffering and frustration.

And, of course, churches that sing black gospel music know it too:

Ain't gonna let no body turn me around, turn me around, turn me around ...

It is no surprise that Martin Luther King, Jr.'s favorite hymn was "Take My Hand, Precious Lord" because he knew we have to be close to Christ when the hard times come. He loved that song, and the great Mahalia Jackson sang it at Dr. King's funeral in 1968.

Precious Lord, take my hand, through the storm, through the night ...

So, there's been one cheer for your college's past, the legacy you are a part of.

And there's been another cheer for you, and all the work you've done—learning to engage the world as part of God's missional movement, thinking Christianly about your work and vocation—integral, not incidental.

Which has brought you to this very day.

But what about this third cheer, a cheer for your future?

If, as Jesus warned, our future includes trouble in this fallen world, what's a son or daughter of Issachar to do?

Should we just give a half-hearted, timid "hooray"? A reluctant praise?

Should we be gripped with anxiety about the dangers of standing up for Christ in our pluralistic society? Times are tough out there; we know that. Should we mute this third cheer, this one for your future in these upcoming precarious decades?

I am here today to say, "No, no, not at all!" We will not mute our cheers!

We college graduate Issacharians love the world, no

matter how messed up it is!

We've been studying the creation itself, and we've seen the very fingerprints of God, under our microscopes and in our residence halls, on our sports teams and in the literature we've studied, in our equations and calculations. This is God's world!

We know the Savior and Redeemer of the world, the Christ who upholds it!

We serve the King of the whole world, who rules with with mercy!

We dare not be glib about it, but we know that to suffer for His righteousness, to be found faithful at our own tasks no matter how small or seemingly insignificant, regardless of the consequence, is the greatest of joys.

We give ourselves today to advancing God's reputation and we re-commit ourselves to use our newly acquired wisdom and skill-sets to advance His Kingdom by serving the world—and *that* is the joy of the Lord.

I say congratulations to you on this fantastic day, this day set aside to honor you. Praise God for your work, and for the support of your families and friends and for all you have learned.

But we need to be prepared, brothers and sisters, we need to be ready.

We need to deepen our discipleship, going further up and further in (as C.S. Lewis put it in *The Last Battle*), trusting God more completely, being eager to learn even more about the Kingdom as we go along.

We must redouble our resolve to be joyful and winsome

and emotionally healthy and spiritually alive. We have to work hard at having friendships and sustaining community —staying in touch with one another, even across the miles if we have to—so that we can be whole people who can offer real wisdom to a hurting world, showing authentic insight to a confused culture. Our Kingdom ideas and Christian principles must be embodied in tangible ways in the specific contexts in which we find ourselves, like true sons and daughters of Issachar. We must, like that famously joyous runner in the movie *Chariots of Fire,* learn to feel God's pleasure as we work and as we play.

So I say, friends, even though we know it will be hard, let's throw our heads back in holy, fearless laughter.

In great joy, go forth.

Go forth trusting God's promises.

Go forth with Kingdom resolve to be God's ambassadors, Christ's agents of reconciliation, His people of shalom.

Go forth in singing,

go forth in prayer,

go forth in love, service, laughter,

sometimes in silence, or uncertainty,

maybe even in tears.

Be prepared to rejoice, even in those tears.

In all our work, in each and every square inch of creation, in every zone of life, let's not just offer three cheers.

Let's say with joy, *Hallelujah!*

Let's *shout* Hallelujah!

Hallelujah!

Hallelujah!

Borger invited you to be open to the idea in 1 Chronicles 12:32 of being sons and daughters of Issachar who "understood the times and knew what God's people should do." Do you consider yourself to be a person who knows both the world and the Word? Do you see a deep, integral connection between faith and life? What do you think it takes to become wiser about the realities of the world and understand our culture through the lens of a Christian imagination? How did you feel when Borger reminded us that this call may lead us to suffer?

What is one step you can take to learn more about how to integrate your faith and your career, developing a uniquely Christian perspective on your work? Is there one person who you think is truly a son or daughter of Issachar? Make an appointment to talk with them about this chapter.

. . . .

Byron K. Borger, along with his wife, Beth, owns Hearts & Minds, an independent bookstore in Dallastown, PA. For nearly 35 years they have sought to offer a wide selection of fine books designed to inspire readers to relate faith to all areas of life. Much of their business is on-line where they serve customers all over the world. They travel often, serving many organizations with book displays, remaining active in their local church.

Byron reviews and discusses new books at BookNotes (heartsandmindsbooks.com/booknotes). He is an Associate Staff of the Pittsburgh-based campus ministry organization, the CCO. As a lad he transitioned colorfully from college without graduating.He eventually enjoyed graduate studies through Geneva's Higher Education Degree program, and was surprised with an Honorary Doctorate from Geneva College, which was the occasion for this address. He was the editor of this book project.

THE THREE
ROADS AND THE
THREE Rs

JOHN M. PERKINS

DELIVERED AT
SEATTLE PACIFIC UNIVERSITY
SEATTLE, WASHINGTON

In Acts chapter 1, after Jesus has been with the disciples about the same time that you have been in this university, about three and a half years or so, He has finished His ministry with them, and He is now fixing to send them into the world to turn the world upside down. He is going to say, "You shall be witnesses unto me." *Witnesses.* That's what Jesus calls us to be, His witnesses.

I think, just for instance, of the problem that we face today in our society regarding the economy. Sadly, the church's voice is often not strong enough to speak to our social and economic greed that has brought the world economy down. And I'm asking here today—where is that prophetic voice? That was the idea, after all. We were to be salt and light in the world; we were to be God's prophetic people; we were to speak truth to society. We in the church have lost that voice, and it is a shame.

You have been in an institution of higher education for four years. Now God wants to send you out to be that witness in society, and He is not going to send you alone. He is going to be with you. That's the work of the Holy Spirit. The work of the Holy Spirit is to be your witness, your guide, your helper. "Lo, I am with you always, even to the end of the world," He promised. And He's fixin' to send His witnesses into Jerusalem, Judea, Samaria, and the uttermost parts of the world, and He has the power, the power to accomplish that. That's the whole idea of the Gospel.

The Gospel is the power of God, it is the love of God demonstrated by Jesus' death on the cross. It is that love that can burn through racial, cultural, economic barriers and bring people to God. In this story in Acts, He's sending them to every ethnic group in the world—those places mentioned represent many different races and people groups. And He's saying, "You shall be my witness. You'll start in Jerusalem."

And they went there. And they turned the world upside down.

Peter could say to the people at Pentecost, "Neither is there salvation in any other, for there is no name under Heaven given among men."

"What must I do to be saved?" they cried out. Peter preached with boldness, "You, the people who put Jesus

Christ to death: you must repent and turn to this Savior, the Lord Jesus Christ." And in doing that, they turned the world upside down. Brutality and suffering and pain couldn't stop them. They entered into the pain of the people of that day as Jesus in His Incarnation did. He entered into our world. He came to His own, and His own received Him not—just like it says in John 1. "And the Word was made flesh and dwelled among us here on earth." Jesus got involved, and so His disciples learned to do that, too.

Jesus healed a lot of people because there were a lot of sick people. He fed a lot of people because there were a lot of hungry people. And he told us to go to those people who have failed in society and whom society has failed. Go to the outcast. Go to the prisons. That's His commission for us as well—to go to those who failed in society. And we should realize that prisons show our own failure in our society.

God never intended that prison be a part of His creation. We live in a nation that has the highest prison rate even though we are the richest nation on earth. It was never conceived that there would be a nation as rich as our nation and as educated as our nation—and now we have the highest prison population in the world! And my community, my African-American community, makes up 14% of the population; and 60% of all the prisoners in the United States come from the minority, from the urban communities of our nation. It's a disgrace.

Somebody is not making that witness to our society the way Jesus wanted it to be made. "You shall be witnesses unto me." If it isn't working well, then how can we be an effective witness as we leave here today? How can you, as emerging young adults and young leaders graduating from this place, be a true witness?

I'm going to submit to you that the Christian faith, and living the Christian life as Jesus presented it, is going down three roads. If we are going to be effective Christian witnesses in society, we've got to make certain that we are on these three roads.

What is the first road?

The first road is the Damascus Road. What is the Damascus Road? That road, that's the road that Saul of Tarsus was going down. He was the original Osama Bin Laden. He was trying to erase all Gentile influence on Judaism. That's what a Pharisee like him did. And he had gotten permission from the high priest to go to Damascus, and, if he found any on that road following Jesus, he wanted to bind them and bring them back to Jerusalem and torture them like he had done to Stephen—to death. But on that road to Damascus, he met the living Savior. On that road, he heard God's voice. It could have sounded something like this.

Saul, Saul, I love you. I love you!

Now, you are aware that that is the central message of the Gospel. Yes, John 3:16 is correct. "For God so loved the world that He gave His only begotten son that whosoever believe in Him shall not perish but have everlasting life."

This love—this love of God in Christ—is life-changing! *"Saul, Saul, I love you."*

Paul is going to say later when he writes the letter to

the Philippians that on that road, God arrested him. He apprehended him. He put His arms around him, and He bound him with His love.

Saul, Saul, I love you, Why you don't love me?

Who are you Lord?

I'm Jesus.

Lord, what would you have me to do?

Christ spoke to Saul, and He said, "I've called you to send you far away to the Gentiles, across racial barriers, to turn them from darkness to light and from the power of Satan to the power of God." And Saul (who changed his name to Paul) could say at the end of his life, "I was not disobedient to that heavenly vision."

As you are leaving here, stepping out into a new life, the first road that you've got to be on—make certain you're on it—is that Damascus Road! Are you on that Damascus Road? On that Damascus Road, your eyes are opened. On that Damascus Road, you hear the voice of God. On that Damascus Road, God tells you what he wants you to do; He calls you to be workers together with Him. That's what it means to be a Christian—to be a worker together with God. Are you on that Damascus Road? Your eyes are open, and the people are out there, waiting. You hear His voice, and you respond to that voice. Make certain you are on that road. On that road, you get a vision for the future. Young people, make certain you are on that road.

That's the first road. Stay on the Damascus Road!

The second road is the Emmaus Road.

If there is any road I would've liked to have been on

with Jesus, it would've been that Emmaus Road. I like Jesus. Jesus was funny—I really like Him. He was joyful. We meet Him on that Emmaus Road after the Crucifixion, and He is walking with two of His disciples who have given up. For them, it is over. It's over. They had been with Jesus during that three and a half years. They'd probably been with Him when he walked on the water. They had probably been with Him when He raised Lazarus from the dead. They were probably out there nearby when they nailed Him to the cross and when the soldiers came and pierced His side and out of His side came blood and water. He was dead. They watched Him as Nicodemus and Joseph of Arimathea took Him and wrapped Him up, getting Him ready for burial. He was dead; He was gone. They were probably with Him when they put Him in the tomb. He was gone.

In the story, it is now Easter Sunday evening. These two disciples are on their way home, and, for them, it's over. It's over. Yes, this morning some women went to the grave and they say they saw a boogeyman or something. They are confused. This is a confusing time. These men say they have given up. They are going home. And they are going down that road, that Emmaus Road. And Jesus, He cracks what strikes me as a joke.

He says, "Why are you folks so sad?"

They reply, "Let me tell you, you must be living on the moon if you don't know what's going on. This person, this Jesus, we thought He was the Christ. We thought He was the Messiah. He came, He healed the sick, He touched the lepers, He even raised the dead! We loved Him.

We loved Him, and now the other day, three days ago, they took Him, and our leaders crucified Him. They put Him to death. Yeah, we knew He was dead, but then the ladies went to the tomb this morning, and they came back, and they said they saw a ghost or spook or something there in the garden. But Jesus is gone."

And they were really, really sad. As they walked along the road, Jesus began to talk to them. He began to tell them about Himself and even scolded them a little, saying, "You're so slow to learn." He began to teach them. The Bible says He began at the book of Moses and went throughout the Psalms and the Prophets and shared with them the story of God, the Kingdom of God, that love of God for His people.

I love that road. I just love that road. That Emmaus road is the road of discipleship. That's the road God calls us to be on, learning His story, learning to follow Him. We have turned Christianity into just "being a Christian," and we have defined what that means for ourselves—but not the way Jesus did. Too often, it has nothing to do with actually following Jesus. The Gospel tells us that to be a Christian is to be like Jesus—involved in the world. We are to be His disciples and follow Him.

I love that Emmaus Road we're on, where we learn how to walk with Jesus. I love that old song that says, "He walks with me, He talks to me, and He tells me that I am His own/ And the joy we share as we tarry there, no other has ever known." That's old school, but it is beautiful and good and true.

Are you on that Emmaus Road? Young folks, as you leave here, remember that you have begun to learn a very important lesson: you have learned how to learn. And now, you are going to follow Jesus and you have enough skill and grace to do it. You have enough to learn how to learn to be a disciple of Jesus Christ and to follow Him and to keep your eyes on Him, on His Word—*on His Word*—and learn from Him. Are you on that Emmaus Road, learning about Him and learning how to walk with Him? That's the road you must be on if you are going to be an effective believer. You've got to be on that Emmaus Road.

The last road, dear graduates, is the Jericho Road.

That's the road He intends for us, the reason He saves us—to go on that Jericho Road. That's why He comes to re-deem us. What is the Jericho Road? It's the road of service. It's the road where we rescue the perishing. It's the road where we see people in a ditch in their pain, and we don't overlook them.

You see, being religious is not good enough. Just being religious is not enough because in this famous story of the Good Samaritan that Jesus told, the priest came down that road and he saw that person in the ditch, and, even though he looked at him, he passed him by. He passed him by be-cause he was probably in a hurry. In my community, he probably would be on his way to the pastor's anniversary or the revival meeting. He would find that person in a ditch and the urgent thing that he has to do would be more im-portant than life itself. The person in the ditch is almost dead, he's hardly breathing. But the minister has another project that's more important than life itself, so he passes him by and leaves him in the ditch.

Then comes the Sunday School teacher, the elder, a Levite. He looks in that ditch, and he says, "It's his own fault. This guy should've known that this is a dangerous road." He faults the victim. "It's his own fault! He shouldn't have been on this road! He should've known that this was a bad road and that robbers were going to be on this road. I shouldn't have to take time to help him. He's bleeding pretty bad anyway, he might have AIDS or ebola, and, if I touch him, then I could get sick. I can't go down that road."

But then, in the story, there's this old mix-breed, this contradiction in thought, this so-called Good Samaritan. That's a mixed race guy; you don't know whether he's black or white. He comes down the road. He's the despised person. And yet, he sees the man in his pain; he really sees him. That's the first thing. "He that has eyes to see, let him see."

You can see what's going on. You can see the misery, you can see the neglect. You can see what our schools are doing to young folks in our urban communities. But we pretend that we don't see. We don't get involved.

Well, this Samaritan guy, he probably heard the groan. The Bible says that, when he got there, he had compassion upon the hurting man. Compassion. Compassion is the first principle for obeying God. You've got to see yourself in the condition of the others—that's empathy. And that condition draws you to the hurting, the suffering, the lonely. So, our Good Samaritan goes to him; he heals up his wounds. He uses his own resources; he gets his own balm. He doesn't start a 501(c) right there (he's actually going to do that later.) He first uses his own resources on the nearly dead guy in the ditch. He is going to try to heal this person; he's going to take care of him; he's going to put him on his own donkey, and he's going to lead this person into the city for help.

This is the Jericho Road. This is the road that, now that you are graduating, you must travel on—that road where people are hurting, where people are unemployed, where people are aching. They need you, and—hear this—*you* really need *them*. You need something to pull passion out of you. You need a cause that is bigger than yourself. If you are going out of here, entering your new careers and new towns and new situations just for yourself, you're going to miss it. But if you're going out there with a cause, with the idea that you must be involved with people who are poor and broken, that's going to pull passion out of you. True redemptive passion comes from God and is inspired by seeing the world's great needs outside of you. And so that Jericho Road—that's the road we all must be on.

First, you have to go down the Damascus Road. That's the road of conversion; that's the road where you meet Jesus. That's the road where His light shines into our hearts to give us a mission for Jesus Christ.

Then, we have to stay on that Emmaus Road to be discipled in the Word and ways of God. We learn about King Jesus, and we learn to walk with Him.

Then he calls us to go on that Jericho Road.

What are we going to do on that road? We need some ideas. That's what the president of the college has said, what most leaders say: "I like new ideas. I like ideas based on good principles." And so we need some good ideas, we need some solid principles. But how do we do it, how do we apply it all?

Well, I submit to you the plan that has been driving me for the last 40 years. I call it the three Rs of development. The first R reminds us that we have to identify with people and their problems. That's where compassion comes in and is further developed. We have to relocate. We have to live among the outcasts and poor and hurting so we can hear their groans, feel their pain, and identify with them. That's the first R: *relocation*. We have a little Chinese poem that we use that says:

> Go to the people
> Live among them
> Learn from them
> Love them
> Start with what they know
> Build on what they have:
> But of the best leaders
> When their task is done
> The people will remark
> "We have done it ourselves."

We go not to patronize people, not to further dehumanize the people, not to further their victim mentality. We go to where the hurting people are to help them gain responsibility for themselves and take some leadership in their own communities. Indigenous leadership development is inherent in the Great Commission. So the first R is *relocation:* living among the people. Jesus came to Earth.

He didn't send angels. He came Himself, and He lived among us.

The second R is *reconciliation*. That's the core idea of the whole Gospel. Paul said, "I'm not ashamed of the Gospel for it, God's love itself, is the power of God." What we have done is that we have put this Gospel into our race and into our culture in a way that it has lost its power, and what we have now is a form of religion that denies the power of God to reconcile those who are in enmity. Many of the wars of the world today are racial, ethnic, or religious. And we must ask, "Where is the church? Where are the believers?" Well, I believe that Seattle Pacific has prepared you to enter into that world of pain, to be real agents of reconciliation.

What is the third R? The third R is what we call *redistribution*. I know people sometimes get upset when I say that. They get upset because they think that I'm saying that we're just going to take all the money from the rich and give it to the poor. (By the way, being so upset and protective of our own wealth may mean we have deified money—we've made it into an idol, as if it is the only thing that really matters to us. Idols are never adequate because there's something bigger than that.) But I'm talking about something other then just giving money away. That's no solution, just rearranging the money. People need more than that. People in the hurting and marginalized communities need more than that.

People need, number one, to know our Savior Jesus Christ who said you shall receive power. Then, we have to help them get some motivation, get some incentives, get some ideas. What people really need is incarnated people living with them. They need reconciliation with God and with others and with their own communities. That's what the Church was supposed to be; the Church was supposed to be the replacement for Jesus Christ on Earth—His body, a collective group of people sharing the gift of the Gospel and sharing their lives with the people who are broken and in need.

So, I say to you young folks—what an opportunity! The world needs you. The world is waiting on you to be His witnesses. Jesus said, "You shall be my witnesses." We need to be on the roads—the Damascus Road, the Emmaus Road, and the Jericho Road. We need good ideas about how to practice the 3 Rs—*relocation, reconciliation, redistribution.*

What a way to send you off, out into the world, with this big vision.

Thank you for giving me this opportunity to talk to you. God bless you.

Perkins challenged us to experience God in three ways, on three roads. He explained that the Damascus Road is where the apostle Paul met Christ for the first time, and that we must also have a real encounter with the Risen Christ. Then he talked about the Emmaus Road where we can learn to walk with Christ, learning about Him and His ways in the Scriptures, day by day. And then he talked about the Jericho Road and the story of the Good Samaritan, where we go out of our way to befriend the hurting and serve the poor. Have you been on those three roads? How might you revisit these three avenues of spiritual formation?

Perkins was also clear that we must use our gifts, talents, and resources for the sake of reconciliation and justice. What might you do to take steps toward becoming more involved in your own community? Make a commitment to investigate what you might do.

. . . .

John M. Perkins is a highly regarded and widely known Christian leader, evangelical spokesperson, and author of many books, including his best-selling autobiography *Let Just Roll Down*. He co-founded the Christian Community Development Association to embody his principles of faith-based racial reconciliation and holistic community development among the poor. His transition from school was made early, dropping out somewhere between the third and fifth grade although he now has several well-deserved honorary doctorates. He speaks, teaches, and preaches internationally, and has served on the Board of Directors of several prominent Christian social service organizations. Born in 1930, raised in the family of share-croppers, he experienced brutal racial injustice, came to Christian faith in 1957, and founded Voice of Calvary in Mendenhall, MS, in 1964. He is one of the most respected contemporary civil rights leaders and has recently written for young adults *Leadership Revolution: Developing the Vision and Practice of Freedom and Justice.*

LAUNCH
OUT
LAND
WELL

ERICA YOUNG REITZ

EPILOGUE

There are two things I will never forget about my graduation ceremony: the unseasonably frigid weather and Jeremy Wingert wondering if he would catch his bus. Some of my roommates slipped on blue jeans beneath their formal regalia just to keep warm. Others stripped their beds of their heavy comforters and lugged them to their shivering parents and relatives who huddled together on the bleachers, fighting the wind as they waited for the ceremony to begin.

I don't recall much about the commencement address or the ceremony itself, but I vividly remember my classmate, Jeremy, sitting on the edge of the plastic folding chair next to mine, holding his stopwatch. As the emcee read the name of each graduate and the individual crossed the stage to receive his or her degree, Jeremy timed the exact number of seconds it took for the exchange to take place. Palms sweating and feet fidgeting, he gathered this same data for multiple names. Beep. Pause. Beep. Repeat. Once he had a fair sample, he counted the hundreds of names that appeared in the program before his own, multiplied them by the average number of seconds it took for each graduate to receive their degree, and then turned to me to say, "I don't think I'm going to catch that bus." He was heading for England, so making his connection was crucial if he didn't want to miss his flight.

With anticipation and idealism, Jeremy was literally on the edge of his seat; he could not have been more eager to launch into life after college.

This picture of my classmate, so ready to exit the gates of university life and enter the world, makes me think of the hundreds of college seniors I have worked with over the last decade, many of them so excited to hop a ride to the next phase of life but not always prepared for the realities that await them—and I'm not just talking about missing a bus.

Life right after college is one of the most exciting times you will experience. It's full of possibility and new-found autonomy: earning money, living on your own, doing work in a field you love. But it can also be one of the most challenging. Even if it's smooth sailing for a short time, some facet of the transition will eventually trip you up, or you'll hit a bump in the road. There may be days when plans don't pan out as you envision or when your expectations don't match your current experience. As you encounter these obstacles, try not to view them as a threat to a life of thriving. Instead, know that flourishing in the next phase of your life is not so much about avoiding rough patches but rather about learning how to properly navigate them.

Although I cannot change the factors that contribute to the challenges of the transition, I can offer a few tips:

BE PURPOSEFUL One of the biggest differences between the undergrad years and life right after college is that things are no longer structured with you in mind. In college, the classes, activities, professors—even the paved paths across campus—are all for *you*. In contrast, the next phase is not tailor-made to meet your unique needs. The onus is on you, and you must muster the full ownership it takes to lead yourself (with the Holy Spirit as your ultimate guide). You will need to be *purposeful* about things like finding friends, choosing mentors, finding a church, and living on a budget. Let me encourage you: *go after it!* Don't wait for things to come to you or for someone else to suggest them, but make an intentional decision to pursue what matters now. Start small, decide what you will do, and be faithful to your commitment. And, if you have a stretch where you have not been intentional or you've messed up, receive grace and begin again.

BE PATIENT As you enter this complex world and start "applying what you know" to real life, be *patient*. Be patient with others, with your plans, with God, and with yourself. Be patient with a world that is not yet as it ought to be. We will feel, as Steven Garber so aptly describes, "the push-and-shove" of this "messy world." Expect this tension, and anticipate that things will take time. Whether it's finding community, adjusting to the workplace, or waiting to become a more sanctified version of yourself, understand that the most important things don't happen in an instant. As you seek to apply "the Word to the world" and the "world to the Word," know that significant contributions are born in small steps of faithfulness. It's okay to fail; it's okay to pay dues; it's okay when certain hopes aren't realized right away. Your twenties are for training—for learning, growing, gleaning, becoming. Don't ever lose sight of the vision you have; but also don't lose heart when things do not come as easily or quickly as you hope. God has a plan and purpose as you practice patience.

BE PRESENT In an age of interruption and fragmentation, our world is desperate for people who are present. May you choose to be present in your comings and goings—listening to others, slowing down, taking breaks from technology—but also in the transitional time itself. You may feel nostalgic for college or expectant for the "next thing," but it's crucial to allow yourself to fully embrace the in-between time. Don't write this time off as unimportant or try to pass through it more quickly than God may intend, even if you find yourself living back home, unemployed, or working odd jobs for a stint. Choose to be *present*—put down roots. Though this transitional time may feel disorienting or distressing, it doesn't mean you need to go somewhere else. There's a good chance you are exactly where you need to be—you just need to allow yourself to be open to all God wants to show you in this time. If you choose to be present, you will stand out in a world that doesn't know how to sit still during a graduation ceremony or in circumstances that carry even more weight.

To this day, I do not know if my classmate caught his connection. Even if he did, my guess is that graduation day was the first of many moments where his desire to forge his way as an emerging adult met with unexpected obstacles, unrealistic plans, or impossible aspirations to do better—because "fails" happen for all of us, *especially* right after college. Thankfully, we do not have to prove ourselves. We are justified by Christ alone, the One who makes us perfect in Him. So, as you push through the gates of college into the next phase of life, may you look at the world with "both eyes" open, and, most importantly, as Richard Mouw reminds us, may you make it all about Jesus—the One who has purposed you, is patient towards you, and is ever present with you in this dynamic time.

....

Erica Young Reitz directs Senior EXIT, a one-year experience that helps prepare graduating seniors for the transition into life after college. She works for the CCO at Calvary Church, reaching out to students at Penn State University, in State College, PA. She is the author of the forthcoming book, tentatively titled *Life After College*—a faith-based guide for transitioning seniors and recent graduates to be published in 2016 by InterVarsity Press. Erica did her own transitioning from Messiah College and has an MA in higher education from Geneva College (with a graduate research focus on the senior year transition).

EXTRAORDINARY BOOKS FOR ORDINARY SAINTS

IT WAS GOOD: MAKING MUSIC TO THE GLORY OF GOD

"Lively, engaging and eminently readable—this book shows that it is still possible to write about music in a way that enriches our experience of it. Above all, it will renew your gratitude to God for making such an art possible."—*Jeremy Begbie*

BIGGER ON THE INSIDE: CHRISTIANITY AND *DOCTOR WHO*

Like the TARDIS itself, the fanatically popular series *Doctor Who* is bigger on the inside—full of profound ideas about time, history, and even the mysteries of faith. This book explores key episodes of the series to discover what light they may shed on the contours of Christian thought.